# CHATS ON OLD CLOCKS

BY
ARTHUR HAYDEN

AUTHOR OF "CHATS ON COTTAGE AND FARMHOUSE FURNITURE,"
"CHATS ON OLD PRINTS," ETC.

WITH A FRONTISPIECE AND 80 ILLUSTRATIONS

Copyright © 2013 Read Books Ltd.
This book is copyright and may not be
reproduced or copied in any way without
the express permission of the publisher in writing

British Library Cataloguing-in-Publication Data
A catalogue record for this book is available from the
British Library

# A History of Clocks and Watches

Horology (from the Latin, Horologium) is the science of measuring time. Clocks, watches, clockwork, sundials, clepsydras, timers, time recorders, marine chronometers and atomic clocks are all examples of instruments used to measure time. In current usage, horology refers mainly to the study of mechanical timekeeping devices, whilst chronometry more broadly included electronic devices that have largely supplanted mechanical clocks for accuracy and precision in timekeeping. Horology itself has an incredibly long history and there are many museums and several specialised libraries devoted to the subject. Perhaps the most famous is the *Royal Greenwich Observatory,* also the source of the Prime Meridian (longitude 0° 0' 0"), and the home of the first marine timekeepers accurate enough to determine longitude.

The word 'clock' is derived from the Celtic words *clagan* and *clocca* meaning 'bell'. A silent instrument missing such a mechanism has traditionally been known as a timepiece, although today the words have become interchangeable. The clock is one of the oldest human interventions, meeting the need to consistently measure intervals of time shorter than the natural units: the day, the lunar month and the year. The current sexagesimal system of time measurement dates to approximately 2000 BC in Sumer. The Ancient Egyptians divided the day into two twelve-hour periods and used large obelisks to track the movement of the sun. They also developed water clocks, which had also been employed frequently by the Ancient Greeks, who called them 'clepsydrae'. The Shang Dynasty is also believed to have used the outflow water clock around the same time.

The first mechanical clocks, employing the verge escapement mechanism (the mechanism that controls the rate of a clock by advancing the gear train at regular intervals or 'ticks') with a foliot or balance wheel timekeeper (a weighted wheel that rotates back and forth, being returned toward its centre position by a spiral), were invented in Europe at around the start of the fourteenth century. They became the standard timekeeping device until the pendulum clock was invented in 1656. This remained the most accurate timekeeper until the 1930s, when quartz oscillators (where the mechanical **resonance** of a vibrating crystal is used to create an electrical signal with a very precise **frequency**) were invented, followed by atomic clocks after World War Two. Although initially limited to laboratories, the development of microelectronics in the 1960s made **quartz clocks** both compact and cheap to produce, and by the 1980s they became the world's dominant timekeeping technology in both clocks and **wristwatches**.

The concept of the wristwatch goes back to the production of the very earliest watches in the sixteenth century. Elizabeth I of England received a wristwatch from Robert Dudley in 1571, described as an arm watch. From the beginning, they were almost exclusively worn by women, while men used pocket-watches up until the early twentieth century. This was not just a matter of fashion or prejudice; watches of the time were notoriously prone to fouling from exposure to the elements, and could only reliably be kept safe from harm if carried securely in the pocket. Wristwatches were first worn by military men towards the end of the nineteenth century, when the importance of synchronizing manoeuvres during war without potentially revealing the plan to the enemy through signalling was increasingly recognized. It was clear that using pocket watches while in the heat of battle or while mounted on a horse was impractical, so officers began to strap the watches to their wrist.

The company H. Williamson Ltd., based in Coventry, England, was one of the first to capitalize on this opportunity. During the company's 1916 AGM it was noted that '...the public is buying the practical things of life. Nobody can truthfully contend that the watch is a luxury. It is said that one soldier in every four wears a wristlet watch, and the other three mean to get one as soon as they can.' By the end of the War, almost all enlisted men wore a wristwatch, and after they were demobilized, the fashion soon caught on - the British *Horological Journal* wrote in 1917 that '...the wristlet watch was little used by the sterner sex before the war, but now is seen on the wrist of nearly every man in uniform and of many men in civilian attire.' Within a decade, sales of wristwatches had outstripped those of pocket watches.

Now that clocks and watches had become 'common objects' there was a massively increased demand on clockmakers for maintenance and repair. Julien Le Roy, a clockmaker of Versailles, invented a face that could be opened to view the inside clockwork – a development which many subsequent artisans copied. He also invented special repeating mechanisms to improve the precision of clocks and supervised over 3,500 watches. The more complicated the device however, the more often it needed repairing. Today, since almost all clocks are now factory-made, most modern clockmakers *only* repair clocks. They are frequently employed by jewellers, antique shops or places devoted strictly to repairing clocks and watches.

The clockmakers of the present must be able to read blueprints and instructions for numerous types of clocks and time pieces that vary from antique clocks to modern time pieces in order to fix and make clocks or watches. The trade requires fine motor coordination as clockmakers must frequently work on devices with small gears and fine machinery, as well as an appreciation for the original art form. As is evident from this very short history of clocks and watches, over the centuries the items themselves have changed – almost out of recognition, but the importance of time-keeping has not. It is an area which provides a constant source of fascination and scientific discovery, still very much evolving today. We hope the reader enjoys this book.

## DEDICATION

Time, you laggard, take my little book,
    And point to those who have a curious mind
    That record herein they may hidden find
Of Huygens' wordy war with Dr. Hooke:
Of David Ramsay's search for secret hoard:
Of Thomas Chamberlaine de Chelmisforde.

Many a maker left his graven name,—
    That by your leave stands yet on dial plate,—
    With legend *Fecit*, of uncertain date,
Proud with the hope that time would bring him fame.
Death stopped the wheels of maker and machine:
Time! will you not their memory keep green?

Time, take my tribute to your flying feet;
    Paper will shortly crumble into dust.
    You guard the guerdon free from moth and rust,
Your even finger sifts the chaff from wheat;
Hold me from hurt, I worship at your shrine
With every pulse-beat,—Father, make me thine.

                                          A. H.

# PREFACE

A PREFACE should be personal. An author who writes on such subjects as Old Furniture and Old China, with a view to educating public taste and attempting to show why certain objects should be regarded more lovingly than others, meets with a volume of correspondence from collectors. Threaded through such correspondence, extended over a long period, I find the constant demand for a volume dealing with old clocks in a popular manner.

There is no house without its clock or clocks, and few collectors of old furniture have excluded clocks from their hobby. I have been therefore blamed that I did not include some more detailed treatment of clocks in my volumes on "Old Furniture" and "Cottage and Farmhouse Furniture," my readers very justly advancing the argument that clocks form part of the study of domestic furniture as a whole.

This may be admitted. But in the endeavour to satisfy such a want on the part of my clients, I plead that the subject of clockmaking is one to which years of study must be devoted.

Since the first appearance of my *Chats on Old*

*Furniture* in 1905, I have not been unmindful of the co-related subject of old clocks. Over ten years of study, running parallel with my other work on the evolution of ornament and decoration of the English home, has enabled me to gather a mass of material and to attempt to satisfy the request for a complementary volume to my *Chats on Old Furniture* and *Chats on Cottage and Farmhouse Furniture*.

To this end I have embodied in this present volume many facts relating to provincial styles as well as Scottish and Irish types, with lists of local makers not before published.

To the critics to whom I have hitherto been indebted for realizing the niche I desire to fill with my volumes, I preface this volume by stating that as far as possible the technicalities of clockmaking have been eliminated. The average reader and the average collector would be bored by such details, although some of us might like to see them included. I have not referred to foreign clockmaking, nor to famous church and turret clocks, nor to marvels of horology; I have advisedly limited my field to the English domestic clock. That such a treatment would appeal more to the collector is my personal opinion, and I trust my critics may incline to my view.

The illustrations in the volume have been chosen to illustrate the letterpress and to illuminate points I endeavour to make in regard to the evolution of the various types coming under my observation.

I have to express my indebtedness to the authorities of the British Museum for permission to include

## PREFACE 13

illustrations of examples in that collection, and I am similarly indebted to the authorities of the National Museum, Dublin.

By the courtesy of the Corporation of Nottingham I am reproducing a clock in their collection, and similarly by the courtesy of the Bristol Corporation I am including an example in their possession. The Corporation of Glasgow have afforded me permission to include a remarkable example of Scottish work, and the authorities of the Metropolitan Museum, New York, have accorded me a similar privilege in illustrating specimens in their collection.

Among those who have generously augmented my researches and come to my aid in regard to local makers, I desire to express my obligation to George H. Hewitt, Esq., J.P., of Liverpool, who arranged the clocks in the exhibit at the Liverpool Tercentenary Exhibition in 1907, and to E. Rimbault Dibdin, Esq., of the Walker Art Gallery, Liverpool. To Basil Anderton, Esq., of the Public Libraries, Newcastle-upon-Tyne, and to T. Leo Reid, Esq., of Newcastle-upon-Tyne, I am especially grateful for solid help in regard to North Country makers. To H. Tapley-Soper, Esq., City Librarian, Exeter, I am indebted for names of West-Country makers, and to A. Bromley Sanders, Esq., of Exeter, I am obliged for information relating to local clocks coming under his purview for many years. James Davies, Esq., of Chester, and S. H. Hamer, Esq., of Halifax, have enlarged my horizon in regard to local makers. H. Wingent, Esq., of Rochester, an enthusiastic collector and connoisseur of old clocks, has kindly enabled me to reproduce one of his examples. To Herbert Bolton, Esq., of the Bristol Museum and Art Gallery, I am indebted for the inclusion of a fine specimen in that collection.

I desire especially to record the generous aid I have had from Percy Webster, Esq., of Great Portland Street, London, who is well known as a connoisseur of old clocks, and from his son, Malcolm R. Webster, Esq., who have given me practical assistance in regard to verifying facts from actual examples.

To Thomas Rennie, Esq., of the Glasgow Art Galleries and Museums, I desire to record thanks. To Edward Campbell, Esq., of Glasgow, who has enriched my volume with examples of Scottish work in his collection, I am indebted for information regarding Scottish makers embodied in this volume.

I am, by the kindness of John Smith, Esq., of Edinburgh, author of *Old Scottish Clockmakers*, and of his publisher, William J. Hay, Esq., John Knox's House, Edinburgh, enabled to produce names and dates of certain Scottish makers not recorded elsewhere. In this connection my friend William R. Miller, Esq., of Leith, has spared no time to help me to do justice to Scottish makers, and I am especially grateful to him for his kindly enthusiasm. He was there at the "chap o' the knok" when I asked his help.

Westropp Dudley, Esq., of the National Museum, Dublin, has extended to me his courtesy in enabling the inclusion of Irish makers coming under his research. To Arthur Deane, Esq., of the Public Art Gallery and Museum, Belfast, I am similarly obliged for data relative to old Belfast clockmakers.

To the many friends who have during an extended period generously supplemented my own studies by supplying me with data in regard to provincial makers and other hitherto unelucidated matters, I wish to offer my cordial thanks.

To my readers in general, whether they be collectors of old English china or earthenware, of furniture, or of prints, or of old silver, I desire to record my appreciation of their kindness in regard to my volumes on these subjects. I have honestly endeavoured to treat each sub-head concerning the evolution of design in the English home with sane reasoning, and I trust with ripe judgment. I have assiduously collected facts and studiously attempted to marshal them, each by each, according to relative value. Popular my volumes may be, but it is my hope that they may contribute something of permanent value to the subjects with which they deal.

ARTHUR HAYDEN.

# CONTENTS

|  | PAGE |
|---|---|
| PREFACE | 11 |
| LIST OF ILLUSTRATIONS | 21 |

### CHAPTER I

INTRODUCTORY NOTE . . . . . 27

Time and its measurement — Day and night — Early mechanism—The domestic clock—The personal clock—Rapid phases of invention—The dawn of science—The great English masters of clockmaking — The several branches of a great art—What to value and what to collect—Hints for beginners

### CHAPTER II

THE BRASS LANTERN CLOCK . . . . 45

The domestic clock—Its use as a bracket or wall clock—Seventeenth-century types—Continuance of manufacture in provinces—Their appeal to the collector

### CHAPTER III

THE LONG-CASE CLOCK—THE PERIOD OF VENEER AND MARQUETRY . . . . 67

What is veneer?—What is marquetry?—The use of veneer and marquetry on long-case clocks—No common origin of design—*Le style réfugié*—Derivative nature of marquetry clock-cases—The wall-paper period—The incongruities of marquetry

## CONTENTS

### CHAPTER IV

THE LONG-CASE CLOCK—THE PERIOD OF LACQUER . 105

What is lac?—Its early introduction into this country—"The Chinese taste"—Colour *versus* form—Peculiarities of the lacquered clock-case—The English school—English amateur imitators—Painted furniture not lacquered work—The inn clock

### CHAPTER V

THE LONG-CASE CLOCK—THE GEORGIAN PERIOD . 131

The stability of the "grandfather" clock—The burr-walnut period—Thomas Chippendale—The mahogany period—Innovations of form—The Sheraton style—Marquetry again employed in decoration

### CHAPTER VI

THE EVOLUTION OF THE LONG-CASE CLOCK . . 153

Its inception—Its Dutch origin—The changing forms of the hood, the waist, and the base—The dial and its character—The ornamentation of the spandrel—The evolution of the hands

### CHAPTER VII

THE BRACKET CLOCK . . . . . 179

The term "bracket clock" a misnomer—The great series of English table or mantel clocks—The evolution of styles—Their competition with French elaboration

### CHAPTER VIII

PROVINCIAL CLOCKS . . . . . 211

Their character—Names of clockmakers found on clocks in the provinces—The North of England: Newcastle-upon-Tyne—Yorkshire clockmakers: Halifax and the district—Liverpool and the district—The Midlands—The Home Counties—The West Country—Miscellaneous makers

## CONTENTS

### CHAPTER IX

SCOTTISH AND IRISH CLOCKS . . . . 255

David Ramsay, Clockmaker Extraordinary to James I—Some early "knokmakers"—List of eighteenth-century Scottish makers—Character of Scottish clocks—Irish clockmakers: Dublin, Belfast, Cork—List of Irish clockmakers

### CHAPTER X

A FEW NOTES ON WATCHES . . . . 281

The age of Elizabeth—Early Stuart watches—Cromwellian period—Watches of the Restoration—The William and Mary watch—Eighteenth-century watches—Pinchbeck and the toy period—Battersea enamel and shagreen

INDEX . . . . . . . 295

# ILLUSTRATIONS

BRASS LANTERN CLOCK BY JOHN BUSHMAN, 1680 . *Frontispiece*

CHAPTER II.—THE BRASS LANTERN CLOCK
                                                                 PAGE

Ship's Lantern of Silver (Danish) . . . . 47
Early Lantern Clock by Bartholomew Newsam . . 47
Seventeenth-century Brass Clocks, showing pendulum at front and at back . . . . . . 51
Brass Lantern Clock by Daniel Quare, 1660 . . 55
   ,,      ,,      ,, with two hands and anchor pendulum 55
   ,,      ,,      ,, with long pendulum, chains and weights 57
   ,,      ,,      ,, by Thomas Tompion (1671–1713) . 61

CHAPTER III.—THE LONG-CASE CLOCK — THE PERIOD OF VENEER AND MARQUETRY

Long-case Clock. Maker, Jas. Leicester . . . 75
   ,,      ,,      ,, by J. Windmills, *c*. 1705 . . 77
   ,,      ,,      ,, enlargement of dial . . . 77
   ,,      ,,      ,, by Henry Harper (1690–5) . . 81
   ,,      ,,      ,, by Martin (London), 1710 . . 85
   ,,      ,,      ,, in marquetry, "all over" style . . 87
Chest of Drawers (William and Mary period), showing use of marquetry clock panel . 93–5

## Chapter IV.—The Long-case Clock — The Period of Lacquer

|  | PAGE |
|---|---|
| Long-case Clock by Joseph Dudds (1766–82) | 115 |
| ,, ,, ,, by Kenneth Maclennan (1760–80) | 117 |
| Inn Clock by John Grant (Fleet Street), c. 1785 | 125 |

## Chapter V.—The Long-case Clock — The Georgian Period

| | |
|---|---|
| Long-case Clock by Henderson, c. 1770 | 133 |
| ,, ,, ,, by Thomas Wagstaff, c. 1780 | 137 |
| ,, ,, ,, by Stephen Rimbault, case by Robert Adam, c. 1775 | 139 |
| Musical Long-case Clock (top portion) | 143 |
| Long-case Clock by James Hatton (1800–12) | 145 |
| Regulator Long-case Clock by Robert Molyneux & Sons (1825) | 149 |
| Enlargement of dial | 149 |

## Chapter VI.—The Evolution of the Long-case Clock

| | |
|---|---|
| Brass Dial by Henry Massy, c. 1680 | 159 |
| ,, ,, by John Draper, c. 1703 | 159 |
| Enlargements of Dials by John Bushman and Henry Massy | 163 |
| English Wood-carving, Cherub's Head (seventeenth century) | 167 |
| Brass Spandrel from Clock, Henry Massy (1680) | 167 |
| Stretcher of William and Mary Chair (detail) | 171 |
| Brass Spandrel of Dial of Clock | 171 |

## Chapter VII.—The Bracket Clock

Bracket Clocks by :—

| | |
|---|---|
| Sam Watson (Coventry), 1687. Joseph Knibb (Oxon), 1690 | 181 |
| Thomas Loomes (London), 1700. Thomas Johnson (London), 1730 | 183 |

# ILLUSTRATIONS

CHAPTER VII.—THE BRACKET CLOCK (*continued*)

PAGE

Bracket Clocks by :—
    John Page (Ipswich), 1740. Godfrey Poy (London), 1745 . . . . . 187
    Johnson (London), 1760. Thomas Hill (London), 1760 . . . . . 189
American Clock by Savin & Dyer (Boston), 1780-1800 . 193
Staffordshire Copper Lustre Ware Vase, with painted Clock Dial . . . . . . . 195
Bracket Clocks by :—
    Alexander Cumming (London), 1770. Anonymous, 1800 . . . . . 199
    Barraud (London), 1805. Strowbridge (Dawlish) 201
    Biddell (London), 1800. Anonymous (1800-15) . . . . . . 205
Ebony Table Clock, decorated with Wedgwood Medallions 207

CHAPTER VIII.—PROVINCIAL CLOCKS

Copper Token, Leeds Halfpenny, 1793 . . . 218
Long-case Clock by Gilbert Chippindale (Halifax) . 219
  ,,  ,,  ,, enlargement of hood . . . 219
  ,,  ,,  ,, by John Weatherilt (Liverpool) (1780-85) . . . . 221
  ,,  ,,  ,, by Thurston Lassell (Liverpool), 1745 . 225
  ,,  ,,  ,, by Henry Higginbotham (Macclesfield) . 227
  ,,  ,,  ,, by Heywood (Northwich), 1790 . . 231
  ,,  ,,  ,, by Thomas Wall (Birmingham), *c.* 1795 233
Copper Token, Joseph Knibb, Clockmaker in Oxon . 236
Long-case Clock by Joseph Knibb (Oxon), *c.* 1690 . 237
  ,,  ,,  ,, Georgian, Spanish mahogany, by Cockey (Warminster) . . . . 239
Brass Dial of Welsh Clock by Shenkyn Shon (Pontnedd Fechan), 1714 . . . . . 243
Iron Dial of Sussex Clock by Beeching (Ashburnham) . 243

CHAPTER VIII.—PROVINCIAL CLOCKS (*continued*)
PAGE
Long-case Clock, with oval dial, by Marston (Salop), 1761 245
Dials of Clocks by Marston (Salop) and Thomas Wall (Birmingham) . . . . . . 249

CHAPTER IX.—SCOTTISH AND IRISH CLOCKS

Brass Lantern Clock by Humphry Mills (Edinburgh), 1670 259
,,    ,,    ,,    do. showing movement    .    . 259
Long-case Clock by Patrick Gordon (Edinburgh), 1705-15 263
Dial of Long Pendulum Clock by Jos. Gibson (Ecclefechan), c. 1750 . . . 267
,,    ,,    ,,    ,,    enlargement, showing maker's name    .    .    . 267
Wall Clock, decorated in marquetry, by George Graydon (Dublin), c. 1796    .    .    .    .    . 269
Musical Clock by George Aicken (Cork), 1770-95    . 273
Regulator Clock, mahogany case, by Sharp (Dublin)    . 275

CHAPTER X.—A FEW NOTES ON WATCHES

Old English Watches (Elizabethan, James I, Cromwellian, and Charles II) .    .    . 283
,,    ,,    (eighteenth-century examples)    . 287
Calendar Watch (seventeenth century) by Thomas Chamberlaine de Chelmisforde    .    .    .    .    . 291

# CHAPTER I

# INTRODUCTORY NOTE

# CHAPTER I

## INTRODUCTORY NOTE

Time and its measurement — Day and night — Early mechanism — The domestic clock — The personal clock — Rapid phases of invention — The dawn of science — The great English masters of clockmaking — The several branches of a great art — What to value and what to collect — Hints for beginners.

THE dictionary definition of "clock" is interesting. *Clock*.—A machine for measuring time, marking the time by the position of its hands upon the dial-plate, or by the striking of a hammer on a bell. Probably from old French or from Low Latin, *cloca, clocca*, a bell. Dutch, *klok*. German, *glocke*, a bell.

This is exact as far as it goes, but the thought seizes one, how did it come about that man attempted to measure time? He saw the sunrise and he watched the fading sunset till "Hesperus with the host of heaven came," and the night melted again into the dawn. Nature marked definitely the hours of light and hours of darkness. That was a law over which he had no control. Similarly he watched the seasons—the spring, the summer, the autumn, and the winter; this gave him the annual calendar. It becomes a matter of curious speculation how it came to pass that man divided the year into twelve months, and how he came to give a name to each day, and to determine seven as forming a week. Similarly one is curiously puzzled as to why he divided day and night into twenty-four parts, calling them hours.

These speculations lead us farther afield than the scope of this volume. An examination of Babylonian and Greek measurements of time is too abstruse to be included in a volume of this nature. Nor is it necessary, however interesting such may be, to record the astronomical observations at Bagdad of Ahmed ibn Abdullah.

We must commence with the known data that the earth revolves on its axis in twenty-four hours, or, to be more exact, in 23 hours 56 minutes 4 seconds. Astronomical clocks recording with scientific exactitude this phenomenon are on a plane apart, as are chronometers used by mariners. The astronomer uses a clock with numbers on its dial plate up to twenty-four; the common clock has only twelve hour numerals.

To come straight to modernity, it must be recognized that the measurement of time scientifically and the measurement of time according to civil law are two different things.

The mean Solar day used in the ordinary reckoning of time, by most modern nations, begins at midnight. Its hours are numbered in two series

## INTRODUCTORY NOTE 29

from 1 to 12—the first series, called A.M. (*ante meridian*), before midday, and the second series, P.M. (*post meridian*), after midday. This is a clumsy arrangement and leads to confusion. The leading railways of the world are beginning to use the series of twenty-four.

Let it be granted that the day consists of twenty-four hours, which is the apparent Solar day; the starting-point was not always the same. The Babylonians began their day at sunrise, the Athenians and Jews at sunset, the ancient Egyptians and Romans at midnight.

In passing, it should be noted that the day is measured astronomically by recording the period of the revolution of the earth on its axis, determined by the interval of time between two successive transits of the sun, the moon, or a fixed star over the same meridian.

The Solar day is exactly 24 hours, the Lunar day is 24 hours 50 minutes, and the Sidereal day is 23 hours 56 minutes.

Apparent Solar Time is shown by the sundial, and therefore depends upon the motion of the sun. Mean Solar Time is shown by a correct clock. The difference between Mean Time and Apparent Time, that is, between the time shown by the clock and the sundial, is called the Equation of Time, and in the *Nautical Almanack*, a Government publication, there are tables showing these differences.

**Day and Night.**—Obviously the hours of darkness offered a greater problem to the horologist than the hours of light. His sundial was of no use at night and of little use on cloudy days. The hour-glass was not a piece of mechanism a man would wish to employ to record the night watches. Some other self-acting mechanism had to be devised.

The interval between sunset and sunset, or sunrise and sunrise, or noon and noon, was divided by the Babylonians, who had a love for the duodenary system, into twenty-four hours. It is curious to read that "until the eighteenth century in England the hour was commonly reckoned as the twelfth part of the time between sunrise and sunset, or between sunset and sunrise, and hence was of varying durations" (*Webster's New International Dictionary*, 1914).

The hour was further divided, also by the Babylonians, into periods of sixty minutes. It was the Babylonians who first divided the circle into 360 degrees, and Ptolemy followed this division.

The dial of a clock was at first termed the *hour-plate*, as only hours were engraved upon it and only one hand was employed. Later, another hand was added, the minute hand, which travelled a complete circuit while the hour hand was travelling between two hour numerals. Later, again, a new sub-dial was added, and a seconds hand recorded the sixty seconds which made the minute. The term "second" was at first called "second-minute," denoting that it was the second division of an hour by sixty. The learned John Wilkins, Bishop of Chester, that extraordinary old savant, writes in 1650: "Four flames of an equal magnitude will be kept alive the space of sixteen *second-minutes*, though one of these flames alone, in the same vessel, will not last at most above twenty-five or thirty seconds."

These dry facts may serve to whet the curiosity of the student in regard to the measurement of time and its origin. They add a piquancy to the clock dial as we now know it. Scientific it is, as one of man's most exact recorders of natural phenomena. That an exact timekeeper should be found in the pocket of every schoolboy would seem an astounding miracle to our ancestors two hundred years ago, or even less than a hundred years ago:

> 'Tis with our judgments as our watches, none
> Go just alike, yet each believes his own,

writes Pope in his *Essay on Criticism* in 1725.

This is a damning indictment of the accuracy of watches in the early eighteenth century, but Dickens in *Dombey and Son* suggests equally faulty mechanism not in true accord with the mean solar day:

"Wal'r . . . a parting gift, my lad. Put it back half an hour every morning, and about another quarter towards the arternoon, and it's a watch that'll do you credit."

That the civil day has taken precedence of the solar day is shown by the recent legislation in regard to Summer Time. "The Sabbath was made for man and not man for the Sabbath," may be applied to the clock dial. By an Act of Parliament, in spite of science and the earth's revolution on its axis, the hands straightway mean something else. It is well that modern clocks have no wise saws and mottoes telling of the unalterable hand of Time; "Old Time, the clock-setter, that bald sexton, Time," as Shakespeare says in *King John*.

**Early Mechanism.**—The problem for the old clockmakers who wished to supplant the primitive measurement of time by candle, by the hour-glass, and later by the sundial, was to produce a piece of mechanism which would in twenty-four hours, the prescribed period of day and night, indicate the flight of time hour by hour.

In rapid survey we cannot pause to enter into details. The first clocks indicated the hour alone by a hand attached to the axis of a wheel. In the twelfth century a new mechanism was added to strike a bell with a hammer, showing the hours indicated by the hand. At first the motive power was a weight acting upon toothed wheels. In the fifteenth century a spiral spring placed in a barrel replaced the weight attached to a string as the motive power. This led to portable clocks of smaller dimensions being possible.

The sixteenth century is remarkable for the great advance by Italian, by Nuremberg, and by Augsburg clockmakers. Striking and alarum clocks, and intricate mechanism showing phases of the moon, the year, the day of the month, and the festivals of the Church, were produced. In the sixteenth century portable clocks received further attention in regard to minute mechanism, resulting in what we now know as the watch. The moment this point was reached, ornamentation of a rich and elaborate character was applied to such objects

## INTRODUCTORY NOTE 33

of art, then only in the possession of princes and nobles and the richest classes of society.

In the middle of the seventeenth century Huygens, the celebrated Dutch astronomer and mathematician, brought great modification in the art of clock-making by applying the pendulum to clocks in order to regulate the movement, "and adapting, some years later, to the balance of watches a spring, which produced upon this balance the same effect as that of the weight upon the pendulum" (Labarte, *Arts of the Middle Ages*).

In old clocks there is a verge escapement with a cross-bar balanced by weights. This was in the top portion of the clock.

When the pendulum was introduced it was first placed in front of the clock and swung backwards and forwards across the face of the dial, being only some six inches in length, and more frequently it is found at the back of the clock, outside the case. See illustration (p. 51) of examples.

As it was easy safely to convert the old form of balance into pendulum form, with hanging weight or weights, this was frequently done. So frequently, in fact, that very few of the old balance movements remain. See illustration (p. 57) of lantern clock with weights and pendulum.

With the advent of the "royal" or long pendulum, the domestic clock came into being.

We now arrive at the first period of the English domestic clock, and from this point a fairly definite record of styles and changes can be made.

**The Domestic Clock.**—This may be said to be

the clock in use in a great house, apart from the cathedral or church clock, the turret clock, or the more public clock common to the gaze of everybody. The nobility employed, on the Continent and in this country, great clockmakers to produce these new scientific timekeepers for use in their private apartments. But there came another phase when the clock visible to the dependent was supplanted by more delicate mechanism of greater value and of richer ornamentation.

**The Personal Clock.**—This was the watch. It was carried on the person. It was the gift of a lover to his mistress. It was a rich and rare jewel of scientific construction, set in crystal, embellished with enamel and other rich decoration. In a measure it supplanted the clock and drove it on to a lower plane.

It demanded craftsmanship of the highest character to create these masterpieces of horology, and the art has been continued in a separate stream to that of clockmaking up to the present day. The watch is not the small clock, nor is the clock the large watch. Whatever may have been their common origin, each has developed on lines essentially proper for the technique. As the clock has developed in mechanical perfection, so the watch has similarly kept in parallel progress towards the same ideal, that of the perfect timekeeper.

A long succession of mechanical inventions is attached to the clock, and similarly the watch has demanded equal genius till both arrive at modernity.

## INTRODUCTORY NOTE

**The Dawn of Science.** — The mid-seventeenth century the post-Bacon period, when Newton became President of the Royal Society, may be said to be the dawn of science in this country. The Aristotelian method of analysis and the practical experiment set men's minds into scientific channels. The scientific clockmaker was the product of this period of restless activity. Science was in leading-strings. Prince Rupert's Drops, so familiar now, were a scientific wonder. Bishop Wilkins and Evelyn, Locke and Dr. Harvey, were all, from different points, attempting to unravel the secrets of nature. The Tudor Age had opened the New World; the next century was left to discover the untravelled paths of science and mechanism. Invention was being suckled by Curiosity. Invention only came to manhood in the nineteenth century.

**The Great English Masters of Clockmaking.**—There is the mythical claim for Richard Harris, who is said to have invented the first pendulum clock in Europe, fixed in the turret of St. Paul's, Covent Garden, in 1640 or earlier. The Huygens pendulum was hung by a silken cord, and the arc described by the bob or weight at its end was a segment of a circle. Dr. Hooke invented the thin, flexible steel support of the pendulum, producing more scientific accuracy. In 1658 he invented the *anchor escapement*, which, together with his spring to the pendulum, in still used, although the "dead-beat" escapement invented by George Graham has supplanted the "anchor" in timekeepers requiring greater exactitude.

In regard to Robert Hooke and his claim to being the inventor of the balance spring for watches, an invention claimed by Christopher Huygens de Zulichem, there is an acrimonious dispute and lengthy correspondence thereon. The Royal Society had published in their *Philosophical Transactions* for March 25th, 1675, the discovery of Huygens, who visited England in 1661 and was made a Fellow of the Royal Society. Dr. Hooke protested. It appears that one of the "ballance double watches" was presented to Charles II and was inscribed "Robert Hooke *inven.* 1658. T. Tompion *fecit* 1675." There is the record that George Graham declared that he "had heard Tompion say he was employed three months that year by Mr. Hooke in making some parts of these watches before he let him know for what use they were designed, and that Tompion was used to say he thought the first invention of them was owing to Mr. Hooke."[1]

To come to the great masters of the art of English clockmaking. In the transactions of the Worshipful Company of Clockmakers it is recorded that "in July 1704 it was by the Master reported that certain persons at Amsterdam are in the habit of putting the names of Tompion, Windmills, Quare, Cabrier, Lamb, and other well-known makers on their works and selling them as English."[2] A committee was appointed to put an end to such abuses.

[1] *Life of Robert Hooke*, by R. Waller, 1705. *Biographica Britannica*.
[2] *Some Account of the Worshipful Company of Clockmakers of the City of London*, by Samuel Elliott Atkins and Henry Overall, F.S.A., 1881 (*British Museum Library*, 10349 gg. 11).

Here then we have five of the leading English clockmakers in 1704, to which we can add George Graham, the inventor of the "orrery," named after his patron, Robert Boyle, Earl of Cork and Orrery, and to make the number up to twenty-five we add the following. These men are in the first flight. Ahasuerus Fromanteel (and the family of Fromanteel, of Dutch origin), the first to introduce the pendulum into England; Edward East; Joseph Knibb, father and son; William Dutton, Matthew and Thomas Dutton, John Ebsworth, John Harrison, J. Grant, Stephen Rimbault, Thomas Earnshaw, John Arnold, Thomas Mudge, Christopher Pinchbeck, William Tomlinson, Justin Vulliamy, and Benjamin and Benjamin Lewis Vulliamy.

In *Old Clocks and Watches and their Makers*, by the late F. J. Britten, there is a list of some ten thousand names of clockmakers, so that examples coming in the possession of collectors can readily be checked by this list. But the fact that a maker's name is not in this directory does not exclude him from recognition as a master, though possibly he may not be one of the great masters.

**The Several Branches of a Great Art.**—The time-keeper—whether it be the scientific astronomical clock, or the chronometer used by mariners, or the modern watch, minute in size but recording time with accuracy, or the bracket or table clock, or the long-case clock—has proceeded on parallel lines of development. These types represent the several branches of the great art of clockmaking.

Clockmakers and watchmakers very soon specialized when the correct standard had been reached, and further inventions effected economy in mechanism rather than drastic changes in principle making for further exactitude. Specialization may be said to have undone clockmaking. We realize that the clockmaker could not cast the brass spandrel ornaments and chase them, or engrave the dial. We do not expect him to, nor did he, lay the marquetry, or become a lacquer varnisher in the cases. We cannot call upon him to cast the bell in the chiming movement, or to make the catgut which is wound around the drum carrying the weights. Nor was he an expert in metal design to pierce the hands and employ delicate ornament in so doing. Perhaps we may forgive him employing a special trade to supply him with delicate springs. But the factory system of the middle nineteenth century began to eat into the vitals of clockmaking in this country as a scientific craft. Makers of wheels, makers of chains, makers of every conceivable part of the movement sprang into being. No one of whom was a clockmaker, and no unit of any such industry could put a clock together. The clockmaker, and even then there is something personal yet remaining, became an assembler of component parts. He certainly understood the completed whole and made the wheels move and the hands record exact and perfect time. That is something, and it is a very great thing too. But how shorn of his former glory is the clockmaker in these conditions!

In this volume we deal with the collecting period,

## INTRODUCTORY NOTE

which is the stage prior to this, but it is possible to look ahead as well as backward. Factory-made clocks will be made, perfect timekeepers without doubt. But there is still the great possibility that the clockmaker may seize his own and wrest the laurels from the impersonal syndicate. To him who can add personality to a clock—that something which parts put together with mechanical precision lack—there awaits a glorious heritage. The soul of the living clock must echo the soul of its human maker. The old masters have left to posterity living organisms which will not die. It rests with the public to say whether they prefer the gramophone to the singer, the piano-player to the accomplished pianist. If the clock of to-morrow is to be a mere soulless machine, the demand will be met. But if it is to revert to that higher plane of the old masters of clockmaking, it is for those who love beauty and truth to make their desires imperative. For the moment, therefore, the study of the old and the perfect claims the loving attention of the collector who sees new lamps, like those which the magician in Aladdin's palace proffered for sale, in place of old.

**What to Value and what to Collect.**—The appreciation of old clocks is a natural gift. To one his mezzotints, to another his Chelsea china, to another his old silver plate. But to all lovers of fine furniture the English clock appeals sympathetically. It has a twofold claim to recognition. It is, if it be a fine old English clock by an English maker, a reliable piece of mechanism as a timekeeper. It is in certain periods representative, in its marquetry or lacquered case, of styles of decoration and design now only equalled by copyists. If it is by one of the leading English clockmakers its movements are unequalled. It stands as a monument to a great scientific craftsmanship now almost extinct. The great English clockmakers of the first flight " were not of an age but for all time."

Roughly speaking, the first twenty-five years of the eighteenth century and the first thirty-five years of the nineteenth century represent two periods when the clockmaker was doing splendid work. The clocks of the intervening period are of value as representing work of extreme carefulness, and are of course worthy of the attention and admiration of the collector.

In the first period a crowd of skilled scientific clockmakers followed each other in rapid succession and brought the art of horology to perfection. During this first period the clock cases and the clock dials came under artistic impulses not since equalled. It therefore follows that for these two reasons the clocks of the first period are most highly appreciated and are of great value.

The second period, that is, the first thirty-five years of the nineteenth century, represents an era of established and sound technique, exhibiting craftsmanship of a high order struggling for supremacy and recognition at a time when factory inventions and factory-made substitutes commenced to dominate not only the art of the clockmaker but other personal crafts. During this time the case and the dial cannot be said to possess the high artistic qualities found in the earlier period. Art was beginning to sink into the Slough of Despond which for half a century characterized most European arts, both fine and applied.

Hints for Beginners.—To set out to buy an old clock is for the tyro like setting out to buy a horse. In the latter case the teeth may be filed and the hoofs pared to give a simulation of youth to which possibly the beast could not lay claim. In the former, added touches would counterfeit antiquity: here a pair of apparently old hands, there an antiquated-looking dial, and an enshrining case of no particular period, but seeming to bear Time's own impress of age, till one is inclined to say, to quote the *Merchant of Venice*: "I never knew so young a body with so old a head."

The following chapters will indicate the outline of a complex and intricate subject. The case, the dial, the hands, all have to be studied with no little skill in comparison and deduction in regard to errors in clumsy repairers or unskilled restorers, who with vandal hands have destroyed the balance of fine work and introduced component parts which are harlequin to the trained collector's eye. This much for the *visible*. Then there is the movement, that is, the mechanism which makes the clock a clock. This is unseen by the average snapper-up of old clocks, or when seen not understood. There are those collectors who stop short in their requirements. A clock is an ornament to a well appointed home, in the hall, in the smoking-room, or in the dining-room. They are unconcerned as to whether it is a timekeeper or a monument, "long to be patient and silent to wait like a ghost that is speechless." One longs to call aloud to such an encumbrance with its dead wheels and its atrophied hands: "Watchman! What of the night?" It is a servant that serves no longer. It is like a poor relation thrusting his company upon his fellow-guests with dumb tongue and a solemn demeanour telling of former glories.

But the sane modern collector wants an old clock not because it is old, but because he rightly has assumed that there are certain qualities of the old clockmaker's art which are not to be found in later periods. Wise in his generation, he places himself not in the hands of a dealer who has sold a thousand clocks, but in the hands of a practical clockmaker who has made one. A trained man having a knowledge of old movements, and to whom they are something more than inanimate objects, will advise the collector. To such a man a clock is something with a soul. To him one goes who will set the silent wheels moving and endow the dead clockmaker's heritage with pulsating life.

But—the word of warning cannot be too strongly sounded to all possessors of old clocks. Every year fine examples of old work are ruined for ever by ignorant repairers and restorers. In their little day they have destroyed movements and parts which can never be replaced. Of all arts, the art of the clockmaker has suffered most at the hands of the modern destroyer of work he does not understand.

# CHAPTER II

# THE BRASS LANTERN CLOCK

## CHAPTER II

### THE BRASS LANTERN CLOCK

The domestic clock — Its use as a bracket or wall clock—Seventeenth-century types—Continuance of manufacture in provinces—Their appeal to the collector.

THE form of the lantern clock is one that appeals to the artist. We love the candelabrum with candles, with its finely fashioned brass forms, Dutch and English. It adds a grace to the interiors of the old masters of the Low Countries. Nobody is especially interested in the gas bracket or the paraffin lamp. There is the picture of *The Doctor* by Luke Fildes, but here the lamp only adds to the poverty and anguish of the scene. It is realistic and had to be there, and it makes a great factor in the lighting. But the chandelier with candles is the most beloved by the artist who inclines to the primitive, as we all do. The electric light must come into art and it does. The lift and the telephone are facts, but they are difficult, naked and unashamed as they are, to clothe with æsthetic drapery. The cubist and the modern pseudoscientific realist revel in incongruities repellent to art. They seize these as their own, and make them in their presentation more repellent.

Happily the clock has not received the attention of the modern sensation-monger. We are left with the heritage of the past undisturbed. He may gibe at the paint and canvas of old masters, he may deride the grace of the Greek in sculpture, but the simple mechanism of the clock symbolizing "the inaudible and noiseless foot of Time" mocks the charlatan of a little day, with oblivion tracking his scurrying heels.

The name of lantern clock may puzzle the modern collector, but its shape followed the lantern of the period, and, like the lantern, it was made to hang on the wall. We illustrate (p. 47) a silver ship's lantern of the period of Christian IV of Denmark, of the late sixteenth century, with the King's monogram. It was doubtless used in the expedition round the North Cape. It is in the collection at Rosenborg Castle at Copenhagen. This lantern shape is found in German clocks of the period, and in English seventeenth-century clocks the same shape is continued. A fine example by Bartholomew Newsom is illustrated (p. 47), showing the early type conforming to the lantern design.

Not only the form but the usage determined the name. The lantern had spikes or metal hooks to hang upon. The clock similarly was affixed to a wall, and we know it as a bracket clock, because, whether on a wall or on a bracket, it had chains and weights suspended beneath it, as it was not

SHIP'S LANTERN OF SILVER.

Used by Christian IV of Denmark on his voyage round the North Cape.

(*At Rosenborg Castle, Copenhagen.*)

EARLY LANTERN CLOCK.

By Bartholomew Newsam (1570-90).

(*At British Museum. Reproduced by permission.*)

# THE BRASS LANTERN CLOCK 49

in its early form capable of being placed on a table.

We think lovingly of it as belonging to a past that is something more than tapestry figures moving in a misty background. To watch the revolving pinions of a Stuart clock is to hear the echoes of the past reverberate. It requires no gramophone to reproduce dead voices, nor a cinema picture to recall bygone incidents and happenings. One can listen to the same monotone calling forth the departure of the seconds that awakened George Herbert from a reverie and beat rhythmically to his carefully wrought verse. The same hand pointed to midnight that beckoned Lovelace from his revels. We are reminded of Justice Shallow's "we have heard the chimes at midnight,"—an old man's boast of rollicking gaiety. The trite engraved words *Tempus fugit* drew a thousand sweet sounds from golden-mouthed Herrick, who sang of fading roses and counselled maids "with Daffodils and Daisies crowned" to make the most of their charms. *Vanitas vanitatum*, all is vanity; the sadness of it all, the flying hours that no man can recall, the long slow shadow that creeps across the grass—this is the message of the poets; and when they pause for a moment from the dance in the sunlight to think of time, it is, Time the ancient reaper with the scythe, who cuts down the young flowers ruthlessly with the fateful sweep of his blade.

**Its Use as a Bracket or Wall Clock.**—Old engravings of clocks and of clockmakers' workshops show clocks on the wall with the weights suspended beneath the brass case. Such a clock usually went for thirty hours. That is, it was usual to wind it by pulling up the chains once a day, a method retained, in long-case clocks of thirty-hour duration, by provincial makers a couple of centuries later in England.

It is obvious that these clocks stand apart from the era of the spring as a driving force, being weight-driven, and are before the introduction of the pendulum as a regulator of the mechanism impelled by the weights.

As timekeepers they never can bear comparison with the later type with the long pendulum. They stand as examples of early clockmaking, with fine brass dials, with artistic appearance, simple and unpretentious, but lacking the real scientific application of further developed principles of a succeeding period.

A clock that could only be used as a bracket clock or a wall clock with weights beneath hardly filled the requirements of an age when domestic furniture demanded luxury and exquisite taste. The personal clock—that is, the watch—offered more possibilities.

The advent of the pendulum came just at a time when the art of the clockmaker required the necessary impetus to carry him to newer and more extended fields. The invention revolutionized the domestic clock.

As to the clocks used by the wealthy classes in England at the year 1685, one recalls the death-bed scene of Charles II as described by Macaulay:

SEVENTEENTH-CENTURY BRASS CLOCK.

With pendulum in front of dial.

(*At British Museum. Reproduced by permission.*)

SEVENTEENTH-CENTURY BRASS CLOCK.

With pendulum behind back plate of clock.

## THE BRASS LANTERN CLOCK 53

"The morning light began to peep through the windows of Whitehall; and Charles desired the attendants to pull aside the curtains, that he might have one more look at the day. He remarked that it was time to wind up a clock that stood near his bed. These little circumstances were long remembered, because they proved beyond dispute that, when he declared himself a Roman Catholic, he was in full possession of his faculties. He apologized to those who had stood round him all night for the trouble which he caused. He had been, he said, a most unconscionable time dying; but he hoped that they would excuse it. This was the last glimpse of that exquisite urbanity so often found potent to charm away the resentment of a justly incensed nation. Soon after dawn the speech of the dying man failed."

It was Bacon who wrote, a century before: "If a man be in sickness or pain, the time will seem longer without a clock or hour-glass than with it."

The question arises as to what particular kind of clock was at the bedside of Charles II that he should notice that it required winding. It may have been usual to wind it at that particular time every morning, being, as it undoubtedly was, a thirty-hour clock conveniently wound the same time every day. But it is more probable that the King saw that it wanted winding by the position of the weights.

**Seventeenth-century Types.**—The idea of the pendulum had been in men's minds since the days of Leonardo da Vinci, but Christopher Huygens, the Dutch astronomer and mechanician, applied it to the clock. At first it was placed in front of the dial and swung from the top. The illustration we give (p. 51) shows an early clock with this device. The pendulum was next placed at the back (see adjacent illustration, p. 51), and later inside the clock.

We illustrate several types of the lantern clock showing its changing form from a slender and graceful clock, with the dial in correct proportion, to the later type, when the dial projected beyond the body of the clock. When the bell was placed at the top and ornamented by a brass terminal, the name applied to the clock was "birdcage," and pictures by the old Dutch masters show birdcages of this shape hanging in ladies' boudoirs.

It will be observed that as a rule the dials are circular, consisting of the hour plate without the four spandrels. But we illustrate an example of a square dial by John Bushman, London, about 1680, with crown and verge escapement, with short pendulum, and alarum with striking and going trains run by same weight. It will be observed that these clocks have only one hand—the hour hand. In the example above mentioned (see Frontispiece), the dial has an inner circle showing quarters of an hour. The hand, as illustrated, has passed one quarter and half of the next; it is therefore about twenty-two and a half minutes past three. There is also an alarum marked with arabic figures one to twelve. (An enlargement of this dial is illustrated p. 163)

The other specimens we illustrate exhibit slightly varying characteristics.

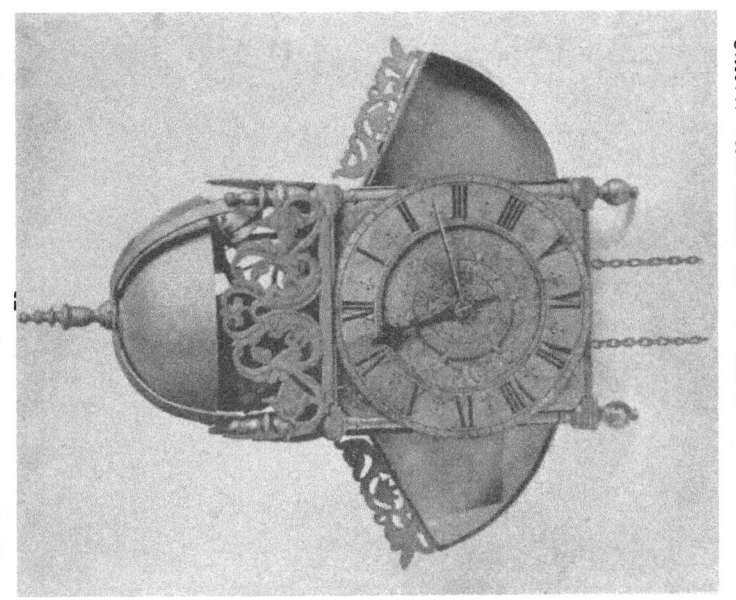

BRASS LANTERN CLOCK, WITH TWO HANDS.

Thirty hours; striking and alarum. Anchor pendulum with wings each side and chains and weight below clock. Short pendulum at back.

Date, about 1670.

BRASS LANTERN CLOCK, WITH SINGLE HAND.

Thirty hours; striking, but no alarum. With chains and weights beneath; short pendulum at back.

Date, about 1660. Maker, Daniel Quare (London).

BRASS LANTERN CLOCK.

Showing chains with weights and long pendulum.
Date, about 1700.

(*At the Metropolitan Museum of Art,
New York.*)

# THE BRASS LANTERN CLOCK

The brass lantern clock illustrated (p. 55) has chains and weights. It is a thirty-hour clock, with striking but no alarum movement. It has a short pendulum behind the back plate.

The use of an anchor-shaped pendulum brought a winged screen into fashion to conceal its movement. The example illustrated (p. 55) shows this style. This also is a bracket clock with chains supporting the weights.

But the bracket clock did not stop at this stage. On the introduction of the long or seconds pendulum this new mechanism was embodied in brass clocks, and the illustration (p. 57) of an example about 1700 at the Metropolitan Museum of Art, New York, shows this type. A fine brass lantern clock by Thomas Tompion is at the British Museum, an illustration of which is given (p. 61).

**Continuance of Manufacture in the Provinces.**—Long after the long-case clock was in general use in London, the brass clock with weights and pendulum was extensively made in the provinces. Examples are found by local makers up to the early years of the nineteenth century. In a measure this continuance of an obsolete form is parallel with the village cabinet-maker's furniture. Generation after generation produced oak chairs and settles in Stuart form, and when Chippendale seized the world of fashion, it was not till long afterwards that village craftsmen made chairs in the Chippendale manner—but in yew, in beech, and in sycamore, never in mahogany. Even Sheraton's satinwood elegance in delicate tapered legs found an echo in elm and beech. It is such naïveté which is delightful to the collector, and in provincial clocks he will find a study equally rewarded by extraordinary anachronisms and singular adaptations within the compass of the local maker.

For instance, the marquetry of the village carpenter is always a hundred years behind the time. His engraving on dials is of the same character as that on his local coffin-plates or his tombstones. His painted dials often exhibit native touches difficult to equal.

**Their Appeal to Collectors.**—Anything that appeals to collectors, whether it be Morland's colour prints or Wheatley's *Cries of London*, old Sheffield plate, Stuart cane-back chairs or Sheraton tea-caddies, pays the usual tribute which the antique pays to posterity. As imitation is the sincerest form of flattery, a thousand replicas start up to supply a demand. The man of taste says that such and such a thing is unique in its art-appeal to him. The man of money seeks to prove that it is not unique and buys as many uniques and antiques as his distended banking account will allow. We find this applies to lantern clocks. Birmingham has turned out thousands of these brass clocks in replica of seventeenth-century styles. Sometimes as much as ten pounds is asked for them, and sometimes it is found that an old maker's name has been added to the dial. There is no particular harm in any man having replicas of fine old objects of art in his house if he likes the styles and cannot afford originals. But it is a pity that any one should ever

BRASS LANTERN CLOCK.

Maker, Thomas Tompion (1671-1713). Height 8¾ inches.

(*At British Museum. Reproduced by permission.*)

pay more than replica price for a copy. That is foolishness, and outside the realm of collecting.

Perhaps it is a wise dispensation of Providence that the man of wealth can possess the originals and that the poor man and the man of taste must content himself with copies. It was Balzac who chalked up in his garret, "Here is a Velasquez," "Here is an Andrea del Sarto." Lovers of the real can impart to the modern replicas purchased for a few pounds the spirit of the old examples. It is the same artistic impulse which accepts the translation in lieu of the original. Through Fitz-Gerald we read Omar. Horatius Flaccus, who appeals to the esoteric with his *odi profanum vulgus*, is filtered through a Western tongue. One is grateful to see plaster casts in the British Museum of the Three Fates from the Parthenon at Athens. Echoes suggest so much to those who have the inner spirit to conjure up the original.

CHAPTER III

THE LONG-CASE CLOCK
THE PERIOD OF VENEER
AND MARQUETRY

## CHAPTER III

### THE LONG-CASE CLOCK—THE PERIOD OF VENEER AND MARQUETRY

What is veneer?—What is marquetry?—The use of veneer and marquetry on long-case clocks—No common origin of design—Le style réfugié—Derivative nature of marquetry clock-cases—The wall-paper period—The incongruities of marquetry.

FOR some fifty years—that is, from about 1670, the date of the secret treaty of Charles II with Louis XIV, to about the year 1720, the early years of the reign of George I—there was a marked leaning towards colour in furniture as distinct from form. The solid English oak of early days and the later intricacies of walnut were dependent solely on form, either in carving or in elaborate turning, as in the Charles II and James II period, when the so-called "barley-sugar" pattern and other elaborate "corkscrew" turned legs added grace and beauty to furniture beginning to take its place beside the work of great European craftsmen.

In flattering imitation of continental schools, but more particularly the Dutch, English cabinet-makers commenced to inlay their furniture with ivory and coloured woods, and designs embodying conventional birds and flowers became of frequent use. A considerable amount of skill was employed in adopting this new art, which necessitated the careful laying of veneer. In comparison with the ordinary Dutch cabinet-work, this derivative English furniture exhibits, in a measure, finished work of a high degree in regard to the exactitude of cabinet-work which surpassed the prototypes. The English craftsman was working in a new medium, and he apparently was exceptionally careful in handling its technique.

In the reign of William of Orange, as may be imagined, with his Dutch retinue and the Dutch influences at Court, the style received a great impetus and the country was flooded with Dutch art. This impress of the House of Nassau is left upon Hampton Court, with its canal, its avenues, and its formal gardens. What Charles II and his exiled cavaliers brought in spirit from The Hague, William brought in reality when he landed at Torbay in 1698.

It must be remembered that in 1685 and in the immediately succeeding ¦years, owing to the revocation of the Edict of Nantes by Louis XIV, fifty thousand Huguenot families fled from France to escape a horrible fate at the hands of their Roman Catholic fellow-countrymen. In vain the Archbishop of Canterbury directed the clergy not to dwell on the sufferings of the French Protestants, and in spite of James II, whose sympathies were with their

## PERIOD OF VENEER AND MARQUETRY 69

persecutors, the sum of forty thousand pounds was collected in the English churches and handed over to the Chamber of London. This was a great sum in those days to be raised thus voluntarily. Three years afterwards James ignominiously fled to the Continent and a second Revolution ended the Stuart dynasty. Thousands of skilled workmen settled in London. At Spitalfields they erected silk-looms; they represented the best type of artist craftsmen, silversmiths, woodworkers, glass-blowers, cabinet-makers, designers, and other artistic industries. Their advent was an artistic asset to this country. The Duke of Buckingham ten years earlier had procured a number of expert glassworkers from Venice and had established the manufacture of glass and mirrors at Vauxhall.

**What is Veneer?**—The art of veneering is of ancient origin. It has a long record before it reaches what we now know as veneering. To make a rapid survey we must commence with the art of inlay. This art may be in metal upon metal, as in damascening; stone upon stone, as in *pietra dura*; porcelain, terra-cotta, enamel, or coloured glass, as in mosaic work; or wood upon wood, as in intarsia; which subsequently became marquetry. The inlays in all these techniques are cut into cubes, hexagons, triangles, or other forms, often of very minute size, to form broad designs, as in marble pavements, or surfaces of great area such as the dome of St. Mark's at Venice, the choicest home of mosaic work in the world. From these grandeurs to the Tunbridge ware trinket-boxes with their intricate patterns, or the nicely fitting lids of Scottish snuff-boxes, is a far cry, but they embody the same principle.

Veneering may therefore be comprehensively described as overlaying or inlaying one body with portions of another. A veneer may be plain, without inlay or marquetry, such as a plain panel of mahogany affixed or laid on to a body of oak or some other wood. But in practice it has been so much used as a groundwork for the art of inlay and marquetry that it is difficult to separate them.

There is a prevalent idea that veneer has a sinister meaning. The comparison has been made between solid and veneer, as though the former were true and the latter something false, parallel with the distinction Pope made—

> Worth makes the man, the want of it, the fellow;
> The rest is all but leather or prunello.

There is every reason why such a notion should be held as true. It is true of modern cabinet-work of the shoddy type, where pine is veneered with mahogany and walnut and passed off as solid. But the collector is dealing with a period when veneering was an art adopted for sound decorative and technical reasons and not solely for purposes of gain.

The old craftsman found it impossible to make cabinets and other pieces of furniture of rare wood, such as ebony, tulipwood, rosewood, satinwood, and others. It was not always workable in such fashion; its weight was one factor against its employment in the solid. But in introducing panels

## PERIOD OF VENEER AND MARQUETRY

and fronts of these richly decorative woods the cabinet-maker of the late seventeenth and eighteenth centuries brought colour into his work and employed the highest artistry. The sound construction of these old veneered cabinets was before the days of machinery; veneers or slices of the wood to be laid on were cut by hand, and were one-eighth of an inch thick, hence their stability. Nowadays sheets of veneer are saw-cut and knife-cut, and with modern machinery the former vary from twelve to fifteen to the inch, and the latter average about forty sheets to the inch, although sheets can be cut, incredible as it may seem, of the thinness of a cigarette paper.

**What is Marquetry?**—Marquetry is the inlaying of wood into wood. We have already seen that other inlays have their respective techniques and names. But there is the question as to the application of the old word "tarsia," which apparently in the early days included both wood and metal inlays. "Intarsia" is the term applied to that particular early type of marquetry which brought inlaying coloured woods to such perfection in two great schools, the Italian and the German. By means of woods, either of their natural colour or stained, woodworkers produced pictures in wood. Great Italian masters drew for the Italian school of artist craftsmen. Just as the dome of St. Mark's at Venice shows the successive styles of mosaic work executed during several centuries from Byzantine to Italian, so the choir stalls show the work of the cloistered *intarsiatori* at the cathedral at

Siena, at the cathedral and at S. Maria Novella, Florence, at Perugia, at Lucca, at Pavia, at Genoa, and at Savona.

Small pieces of carefully selected wood were inserted into darker wood panels to produce fanciful devices or pictures, with perspective and even tone. This intricate art resembled that of the mosaic-worker, whose more ambitious works have taken from fifteen to twenty years to execute. Some of the tesseræ in this technique are hardly larger than a pin's head. Day by day they were patiently laid on the cement to form the design. Similarly in the old intarsia days the workers did not heed time. They selected their delicate little pieces of coloured wood and proceeded to lay their panels and stalls for posterity.

The German school of the sixteenth and seventeenth centuries attracted considerable attention, at Nuremberg, at Augsburg, at Dresden, and at Munich. In North Germany intarsia was principally employed on smaller articles, such as cabinets, chairs, coffers, although Lübeck and Danzig furnish fine examples in the panelling of the town-halls. In South Germany, in closer touch with Italian influence, the practice was more diverse; sideboards, doors, bedsteads, panelling, friezes, and even gables to châteaus, received this ornamentation.

Augsburg and Nuremberg developed an industry and exported their marquetry. This suggests the first attempt at duplication. Black on white and white on black, male and female as they are termed in the trade, or later, in France, Boulle and counter-

Boulle, were exported. The slicing of design and the manipulation of the knife, and later the saw, came into operation to fret out the pattern. In its subsequent development marquetry left the inlaying, piece by piece, and as tools became more perfect easier methods were employed. Whether André Boulle, in his *atelier* under Louis XIV, invented the process or whether he got it from Germany through Holland is immaterial to the present argument. His brass and tortoiseshell marquetry set a fashion to all succeeding craftsmen. He has given his name to his particular style; though it has been "defamed by every charlatan and soiled with all ignoble use" and corrupted to "Buhl," but there is no reason why *Boulle* should not stand, although Webster's Dictionary knows him not.

Practically, nowadays marquetry is the cutting of thin sheets of wood which have been superimposed upon each other, and when taken apart, after the desired pattern has been cut away, fit into each other to produce the desired colour effect. For instance, a sheet of walnut, dark brown, placed over a sheet of sycamore, light yellow, has a pattern pasted on it in paper. The delicate fret-saw traces this pattern and cuts through both light and dark woods. The result is that the light-wood surface is left with a perforation ready to receive the piece cut from its fellow, the dark wood, and *vice versa*. That is just what the marquetry-worker does. He transposes the piece of sycamore to the walnut surface and fits it in, showing a yellow design on dark brown, and similarly the walnut piece, fitted in place or the sycamore ground, shows a brown design on a yellow surface. This is only a simple outline of the process, as more than two sheets are placed together. In its intricacies it represents one of the most delicate and highly skilled crafts in connection with cabinet-making. The adept at jig-saw puzzles may draw a seemly parallel between his pastime and the patient artistry of the artist-craftsman.

**The Use of Veneer and Marquetry.**—In its decoration and in its form the long-case or "grandfather" clock is as Dutch as the tiles of Haarlem. Derivative as is English art, the sharp line of a new introduction is rarely so clearly defined as in the instance of the late seventeenth-century long-case clock. As a long wooden case it was itself an innovation. Being new, it was never at any previous time English, and it started its history under Dutch auspices, as in similar manner the pendulum was introduced into England by Fromanteel. There is no mistaking its origin. It comes straight from the placid canals and waterways, the prim and well-ordered farmsteads, or the richly loaded burghers' houses of the Low Countries. It has become as thoroughly English as the Keppels and the Bentincks.

In regard to clock-cases, it is mostly found that the veneer has been laid upon an oak body. Usually the main surface is of walnut, into which the design has been inlaid by the use of other woods of suitable colours. At first the marquetry

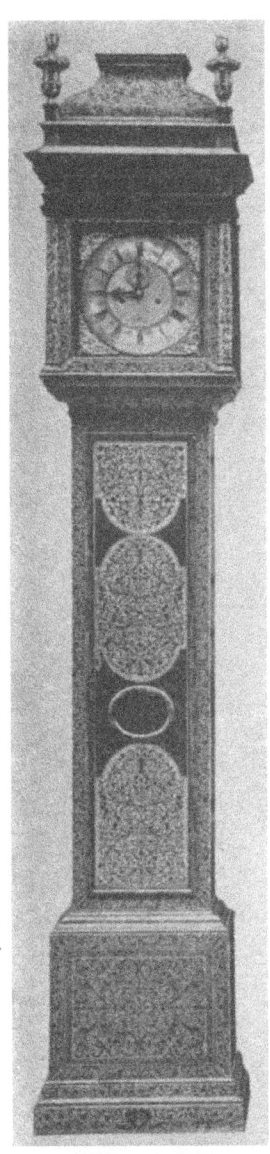

LONG-CASE CLOCK.

With fine marquetry decoration.
Maker, Jas. Leicester (Drury Lane).
1710.
Height, 8 ft. 2 in.   Width, 1 ft. 7½ in.
Depth, 10 in.

(*By courtesy of Percy Webster, Esq.*)

ENLARGEMENT OF DIAL.

Showing cherub's head with floriated design in spandrel and broken frieze. Marquetry in hood indicates coarser style than in rest of clock.

LONG-CASE CLOCK.

Maker, J. Windmills (London). Date, about 1705. Decorated in marquetry.

(*By courtesy of H. Wingate, Esq., Rochester.*)

## PERIOD OF VENEER AND MARQUETRY 79

was in reserves or panels, as though the worker were warily picking his way and timidly mastering the technique. At this period clock-cases were, on account of the small space to be inlaid, very fit subjects for experiment. Doubtless some of the more ambitious work of the early years of this half-century (1670-1720) was actually produced by Dutch and also by French workmen settled in this country, and doubtless the clock-cases were largely imported. In either instance this would account for the early adoption of small articles such as clock-cases, after which followed chairs and tables, and finally larger pieces of furniture such as bureaus, when the cabinet-maker was master of the new art of laying veneer and marquetry, or when the public taste had advanced sufficiently to induce him to embark on more elaborate work.

It is not easy to lay down any exact rules as to the priority of certain styles of marquetry. Many of them overlap in regard to date. It all depends on the point of view. Huguenot craftsmen or Dutch marquetry-workers could, and possibly did, make in London many such an example as the fine case with panels (illustrated p. 75) containing the movement by James Leicester, in date 1710, or the other example, in date about 1690 (illustrated p. 237), with the movement by Joseph Knibb, of Oxford, placed in the chapter on provincial makers as a glorious tribute to those great makers who worked outside the metropolis. In this earlier case of the Knibb clock it will be seen that there are only two panels, and they exhibit, in comparison with the James Leicester clock, a finer sense of proportion in relation to the surface to be decorated. It may not unreasonably be advanced, where the nicety of balance is well sustained, that the maker set out to make a clock-case with the dimensions fully before him as a marquetry-worker and not merely as a mechanical layer of imported panels. There is the suggestion in cut panels that they were not thought out in accord with the English clock-case, with its hole showing the pendulum.

Of exceptional interest is the fine clock by J. Windmills. The marquetry case of this clock has been untouched, and its condition, as shown by the illustration (p. 77), helps to prove a point. It is clear that the panel of marquetry was not intended by the craftsman who laid it to have a hole to show the pendulum. The design shows the disturbance caused by this unexpected innovation. The enlarged hood shows the broken frieze, an accident frequently attending old examples. But the frame in hood around glass has been laid in marquetry by a coarser hand in an attempt to be in keeping with the panel of the door in case below. The somewhat clumsy joinery of the door frame, shown clearer in the enlargement, indicates the amalgamation of the English case-maker and the more finished marquetry-panel worker.

Frequently cases offer curious obstacles to preconceived ideas. Take, for example, the fine case with the movement by Henry Harper of the period from 1690 to 1695 illustrated (p. 81). As far as it is possible to determine, it would seem that this

LONG-CASE CLOCK.

Maker, Henry Harper (Cornhill).
1690–95.

Height, 8 ft 6 in.   Width, 1 ft. 7½ in.
Depth, 10 in.

(*In the possession of Mr. John Girdwood, Edinburgh.*)

# PERIOD OF VENEER AND MARQUETRY

specimen of marquetry belongs to a later period, certainly more advanced than the panel period. With so fine a field of design to select from, no marquetry-worker would take this design from a Persian carpet at the beginning of the style. This case represents the highest Dutch feeling and technique as assimilated in this country, and the carved brackets have a distinctly Marot character. It stands as a superlative example of marquetry decoration.

It sometimes happens that a clockmaker, as the differences in sizes of many of these clocks are not great, found an earlier case ready to his hand, or a client desired a particular style of decoration, and he accordingly put his new clock of 1710 into a case twenty or thirty years earlier. Or it may be that some marquetry-worker reproduced the former style. Whichever may have happened we cannot say—these are the conundrums left as a heritage to the collector, who now comes two hundred years later.

The fine example of a clock by Martin, London (1710), illustrated (p. 85), is well balanced, and typifies the marquetry in an early period. The turned pillar has not yet disappeared, and is reminiscent of the fine Tompion cases with turned pillars. It exhibits the transitional stage before marquetry entirely supplanted the older style. In this specimen the marquetry is under fine artistic control.

In what for convenience of expression we term the "all-over" period the marquetry-worker ran riot. Not only in colour, for he had to compete with the richly coloured lacquered cases, but in form. But he had as a craftsman learned the art of laying his imported marquetry sheets where he willed. He was not deterred from rounded surfaces, and the cramped pattern of the panel was discarded, to make way for the style where the pattern, like chintz or wall-paper, conveniently repeated itself.

There is no mistaking such an example, splendid though it is, as exemplifying this period illustrated (p. 87), for the quieter and more reticent style of panel-work with design in due subjection.

The student will desire to take cognizance of country-made marquetry cases. Marquetry was practised in England before this outburst of colour and form on the clock-case. Occasionally settles and buffets—very occasionally—had stringing in a thin pattern of black and white intarsia work. Provincial makers are therefore a delight as well as a confoundment to the collector. A cabinet-maker in Devonshire or a would-be marquetry-worker in Cumberland may, between his intervals of making the coffins for his deceased neighbours or turning their wagon shafts, essay to try his hand at imitating the squire's clock-case of fifty years' previous date. He usually puts a label to his handiwork which renders it easily recognizable. There is no *style réfugié* about his craftsmanship. His design is crudely "chopped in," that is, the solid wood has been cut out to receive the pieces of the design, usually, as found now, very badly glued, and severely handled by time. This is interesting as showing 'prentice work—that is,

LONG-CASE CLOCK.

Maker, Martin (London). 1710.
Finely decorated in marquetry, with turned pillars in hood. Showing transitional period.

(*In the possession of Mr. John Girdwood, Edinburgh.*)

LONG-CASE CLOCK.

Decorated in marquetry in the "all-over" style.

*(By courtesy of Messrs. A. B. Daniell & Sons.)*

## PERIOD OF VENEER AND MARQUETRY 89

'prentice work coming many years after the finished art had been established in this country. It is remarkable that no such apprentice work appears in London-made examples. The conclusion to which one must come is that there was no such apprenticeship. Foreign refugees made the clock-cases or they were imported from Holland.

**No Common Origin of Design.**—All art is derivative. It is not a crime for the craftsman to assimilate the best of all the great artists who have preceded him. This was the insanity of *L'Art Nouveau*. It wanted to commence again at elementary principles and to use poor forms that had long been discarded by great artificers. It wished us deliberately to ignore the past. An anvil has arrived by a process of evolution through long centuries of metalworkers, since man first smelted ore and fashioned metal, to its present form. It would be idle to equip the blacksmith with a square anvil.

From China to Japan, from India to Armenia, from Bagdad to Cairo, from Alexandria to Venice, from Canton to Goa and thence to Lisbon, backwards and forwards across the world's trade routes art impulses have throbbed to the tune of the monsoons. Pulsating with life, they carried, and still carry, Eastern ideas to the West, and Western inventions to the East. Behind modernity and man's latest devices somnolently lies the great dead past —China and the Far East, Persia and Babylon, Egypt and Greece and Rome. Aztec gods and Ashanti gold ornaments, Peruvian Inca clay vessels and Malayan idols, surprise and bewilder the ethnologist with the similarity of rudimentary forms or with the marvellously pure ornament that comes out of the so-conceived dark corners of the earth to suggest older civilizations as artistic as those of the modern world.

**Le Style Réfugié.**—The history of art is not hidden. Holbein and Hollar and Vandyck, Lely and Kneller worked in this country. The number of foreign artists and artist-craftsmen working in this country as acclimatized or as "naturalized" was stupendous. The beautiful swags and delicately carved woodwork embellishing so many English houses and proudly held as heirlooms are by a Dutchman's hand—Grinling Gibbons. The list could be extended. It is natural that the gold of England should have a hypnotic attraction to artistic temperaments. It is the law of supply and demand. Like bananas and pineapples, oranges and dates, foreign talent comes to a great emporium.

The *style réfugié* was something definite. It was a term employed in Holland just at the time when a similar immigration was occurring in this country. The French Protestant refugees fleeing from the insane fury of Roman Catholic bigots naturally fled to Protestant countries—to England, to Holland, and to Germany. It is admitted on the Continent that these highly skilled artist craftsmen had an influence on the art of the country of their adoption. It is acknowledged as *le style réfugié*. In England, writers on furniture have half-heartedly alluded to this influence, but it was very real. Daniel Marot, a descendant from an eminent family of French

# PERIOD OF VENEER AND MARQUETRY 91

artists, a pupil of Lepautre, formerly at the Gobelins factory, and one of the creators of the Louis Quatorze style, took refuge in Holland, where William of Orange appointed him as Minister of Works. From The Hague he followed his patron to England at the "Glorious Revolution." It was his genius in design that made our William and Mary and Queen Anne styles. At Hampton Court his personality predominates. Sir Christopher Wren occupied himself with the architecture, but the decorations are by Daniel Marot. Marot died in 1718. He stands in the forefront of the exponents of *le style réfugié*, and behind him are hundreds of his compatriots. It is idle to ignore this influence.

Chippendale owed more than most people imagine to Marot. *Le style chinois* is to be found, so to speak, in embryo, in Marot's design books, and suggestions of it appear in some of his executed work.

The un-English marquetry became acclimatized, and later, as we shall show, the equally un-English lac became a fashion.

**Derivative Nature of Marquetry Clock-cases.**—The laying of marquetry as a craft is one thing, the conception of marquetry as a creative art is another. We may admire the dexterity of the inlay but deplore the design. At the Mortlake tapestry works Vandyck and Rubens made drawings for the craftsmen. In England, whenever the craftsman has been allied with the artist he has produced great results; whenever he has run alone he has rapidly run downhill. Josiah Wedgwood had on the one side Bentley the classical scholar, on the other Flaxman the artist and modeller with a perfect continental training. Chippendale, great craftsman that he was, would have been better advised to prune his Chinese taste and discard his worthless Gothic style. An artistic brain behind him would have saved him from such atrocities. Sheraton, more the artist than the craftsman, made no such blunders.

Evidently the making of clock-cases became an industry. Personally we incline to the belief that seventy-five per cent. of them were of foreign manufacture, either in Holland and imported here, or made by Dutch immigrants or French refugees in this country. The derivative nature of their design tells its own story. It has nothing English about it. Take the early geometric star pattern or the early coloured birds and flowers, what else are they but Dutch? Is there anything in English art like them? The conclusion to which one must arrive is that the marquetry clock-case panel is Dutch or Anglo-Dutch. The derivative character runs through the whole gamut from the reticent and well-balanced panel period to the "all over" phase, when every inch was covered with marquetry, to the arabesque and intricate mosaic work reminiscent of Persia, and finally to the decadent period when Eastern carpets found themselves reproduced in marquetry on the clock-case.

When the hood of the clock-case became arched and the dial correspondingly had a lunette, the

WILLIAM AND MARY CHEST OF DRAWERS.

On original stand. Decorated in marquetry. Side showing panel in common use by cabinet-makers and clock-case makers.

(*By courtesy of Messrs. Hampton & Son.*)

CHEST OF DRAWERS DECORATED IN MARQUETRY.
Side showing panel in common use by cabinet-makers and clock-case makers.
(*By courtesy of Messrs. A. B. Daniell & Sons.*)

decorative marquetry panel in the case below followed the same form. It is possible, indeed very probable, that many such shaped panels were imported and were especially intended to meet the demand for use on clock-cases. It is always possible to a trained eye to see whether a panel has been made to fit the place in which one finds it. Is it part of a sanely conceived decorative scheme, or was it used because it happened to be handy as part of a cabinet-maker's stock-in-trade? We illustrate two examples of marquetry chests of drawers of the William and Mary period which offer many interesting features. In regard to the example with the oval panels (illustrated p. 93), the side of the piece exhibits a panel that is incongruous where it is. It is a clock-case panel. Similarly in the "all-over" marquetry chest of drawers of the same period (illustrated p. 95), the panel at the side is undoubtedly a clock-case panel. To examine both these chests of drawers in detail is to discover that the former shows that the panels of the drawers were carefully thought out before execution. The metal drop-handles in the centre were each intended to be there. They were in the cabinet-maker's mind when he made his design and laid his marquetry. He has accommodated his pattern to receive these handles. In the other example it is seen that no such care was taken. The escutcheon of the locks covers a portion of the marquetry. The cabinet-maker in London had his Dutch-imported panels ready to hand and he used them as he found them.

If some collector or expert were to come along and

determine that all the green and purple and flecked glass of the Early Victorian period, bottles with long necks and gilded stoppers, in English leather cases, vases of inimitable colour but execrable form, were typically English as representing early nineteenth-century glass, we should put his theories aside as nonsense. Partly because we happen to know what Bohemia was exporting and partly because we know what the English glassworkers were doing in the same period. But in regard to 1650 to 1700 it is less easy to determine whether a wonderful school of expert marquetry-workers existed in London as a secret industry. One must assume that they had quietly assimilated all the technique of the Dutch craftsmen, and descended on the town, just at the right moment, with a new art, quite un-English, just at that moment when Dutch fashions were in the ascendant and when Mary, the consort of William of Orange, was employing Marot, the late Surveyor of The Hague, to convert Hampton Court from a Tudor into an Anglo-Orange palace.

On an examination of delft earthenware of the period and Dutch decorative art in general, it is fairly obvious that the art impulses coincide with the various phases of ornament as found on the marquetry panel, whether they were the floriated designs of Italy with the vase and the symmetrical flowers in conventional form, further conventionalized by the Dutch, who clung to tulips and carnations, or the arabesque designs derived from the Dutch traffic with the East Indies, the pseudo-Persian sherbet tray

## PERIOD OF VENEER AND MARQUETRY

as a panel, the prayer rug as a full design. With his black delft to imitate lacquered work of Japan and his blue delft to imitate the Kang-he Chinese porcelain, the Dutchman proved himself a superlative translator. The Dutch East India Company, till it was supplanted, was the conduit-pipe through which the arts of the East were allowed to pass into Europe.

In another portion of this volume we show how apparently obscure ornament has a long lineage, and that craftsmen in minor details were producing something of which possibly they knew not the origin nor the significance; but it behoves the intelligent collector, who, after all, is in possession of more facts, spread over a wider area, to arrive at sane conclusions in regard to workers who wrought better than they thought.

**The Wall-paper Period.**—It was a sad time when the idea originated to make wall-paper simulate marble or tapestry or leather, or anything else. Wall-hangings made of paper by the Chinese came into England in the early seventeenth century. But European wall-paper is a modern abomination. Chintz has a better excuse to imitate satin. "Callicoes" were tabooed at first, but they had and have a legitimate place. Wall-paper is an affectation which cannot be defended. It always pretends to be what it is not. It is really wonderful that amateurs did not paste it over clock-cases. Perhaps they did, and other persons, wiser in their generation, removed it.

But if wall-paper of the late seventeenth and early eighteenth centuries was not affixed to the clock-case, it was there in spirit, as it was on strident bureaus and other equally offensive articles of the period. The "all-over" style exhibits marquetry run mad. Artisans could apply the thin veneer, ten sheets to the inch, like paper, and they did. They had borders as common as modern factory-made imitation lace at a few pence per yard, and they laid them beside the pilasters and around the already well covered case. There was no square inch that could be said to be free from the attentions of the gluer of marquetry sheets. He began to dominate decoration till happily he was extinguished.

**The Incongruities of Marquetry.**—To those who have handled a good many examples of marquetry furniture in which panelling is predominant, such as clock-cases, there is one feature which always strikes the practised eye. The question arises, How did the marquetry panel come there? It is another way of expressing the view that the proportion is radically wrong. A glance at a poor panel of a clock-case, or a faked panel, or a stupidly wrought panel, is enough. To the collector of old books nothing is more annoying than to find that the binder with all his fine tooling has trimmed off the margins of the printed matter and the illustrations. It is an edition with the space expurgated. It is the binder *versus* the printer, and similarly in the clock-case it is too often the cabinet-maker *versus* the designer of the marquetry panel. This is the sentiment one has on looking at many of the marquetry clock-cases. The persons who received them from Holland did not always know how to use them correctly.  They either cut off their edges or left so little space as to convey the idea of a curtailed edition of the original.  In the case of the panelled period, when there were three panels, two of them had more often than not to be cut off in the middle to make room for the circular aperture in the door showing the swinging pendulum.  When the case-maker received his panels according to order from the Continent, one would have thought he would have done away with the hole in the case.  But perhaps the clockmaker insisted otherwise.  At any rate, it is a point showing the absence of intimate relationship between clockmaker and casemaker.  Holland seems to be the answer, in spite of all experts to the contrary.

On the "all-over" marquetry clock-cases there is a decided inclination to follow the designs found on contemporary delft ware.  As to repetition, however well joined they are, the glue and the wax cannot hide the poverty of design.  Twice or thrice in one case are patterns repeated.  It is the wall-paper artist at work in a smaller area.  In this connection one recalls the decadence of the wood-engravers, where three or four artists worked on portions of one picture cut into sections and screwed together as one block.  The old journals, the *Illustrated London News*, and the *Graphic* and others of the early 'eighties, tell of this decadence.  The thin white lines, as long as ink and paper last, record this subterfuge.  It was the last note of wood-engraving.  Similarly, in marquetry, when we find the almost invisible lines denoting several hands, or the piecing together of the same design cunningly to deceive the persons at the period, we at a later stage read this as the note determining the end, and the end soon came.

# CHAPTER IV

# THE LONG-CASE CLOCK
# THE PERIOD OF LACQUER

# CHAPTER IV

## THE LONG-CASE CLOCK—THE PERIOD OF LACQUER

What is lac?—Its early introduction into this country—"The Chinese taste"—Colour versus form—Peculiarities of the lacquered clock-case—The English school—English amateur imitators—Painted furniture not lacquered work—The inn clock.

LACQUERED work is the most un-English style of decoration that has ever been employed by the cabinet-maker in the embellishment of his furniture. It came from the East and was introduced into this country about the same period as tea-drinking. At first tea was drunk by fashionable folk from cups without handles, now it is the national beverage. Lac is a natural product of China, the sap of a tree in appearance resembling our ash-tree. It is not an artificial compound of resin and oils, worked down by turpentine. This natural gum is refined and coloured red, black, golden yellow, green, or grey. The surface of the wood is carefully prepared, and a ground is laid on by degrees, care being taken that each is of the right temperature and perfectly hard and dry before any layer is applied. Never less than three and sometimes as many as eighteen thin layers are thus applied to the surface of the wood before the actual decoration of this ground by the artist commences. In regard to the use of lac in this country, practical experts have questioned as to whether it is possible in a climate like this to effect the clean drying so necessary to attain perfection. London and other cities, on account of their dust-charged atmosphere, are unsuited for lacquer work.

The artist draws his design of landscape or figures or birds or flowers, filling his details with gold or silver and superimposed colours built up with mastic, of those parts which are intended to be in slight relief.

The Japanese brought the art of lacquer to the highest perfection. To those readers who desire to see the art of lacquer shown in its various stages, there is in the Botanical Museum at Kew Gardens a collection of specimens in various stages, including sections of the lacquer-tree, from which the lac exudes, and of various coloured lacs, and examples illustrating no less than fifty different methods of lacquering sword-sheaths.

An examination of lacquer work is to be found in *Chinese Art*, vol. i, by Dr. Stephen W. Bushell, formerly physician to His Majesty's Legation at Peking. In the print-room of the Imperial Library at Paris is an album with drawings of the processes and explanatory notes.

The Lacquer Industry in Japan forms a Report of His Majesty's Acting-Consul at Hakodate

## THE PERIOD OF LACQUER

(Mr. J. J. Quin), printed as a Parliamentary Paper in 1882.

**Its Early Introduction into this Country.**—At first the Portuguese had the monopoly of trade with the Far East. When Philip of Spain annexed Portugal in 1598, he sought to shut out the Dutch traders from participation in this trade. By this act he laid the foundation of the Dutch East India Company. It was only when Cornelius Houtman procured some Portuguese charts that the Dutch navigators first rounded the Cape *en route* for India and China and Japan. The great Dutch East India Company was established in 1602.

Porcelain and lacquered cabinets and boxes were thus at an early date distributed as rare articles of curious art at the beginning of the seventeenth century. Drake and Raleigh had captured Spanish galleons with such treasure, and the Portuguese possession of Goa in India had brought the wealth of the Far East to Western Europe. Evelyn tells us in his *Diary*, in 1681, of the richness of the apartments of the Duchess of Portsmouth at Whitehall. "The very furniture of the chimney was massy silver. The sideboards were piled with richly wrought plate. In the niches stood cabinets, the masterpieces of Japanese art." The dowry of Queen Catherine of Braganza did not come up to the expectations of the spendthrift Charles, although she came loaded with "japanned" boxes and rare artistic treasures from the East. Memoirs of this time furnish abundant proof that lacquered work was, in pieces of imported furniture, known in this country.

But it is little likely that anything of that nature was manufactured here at that date. As a nation we had not developed on those lines; it is a fact worth remembering that as late as the reign of Charles II the greater part of the iron used in this country was imported from abroad.

"**The Chinese Taste.**"—This is a term which finds itself repeated like a parrot-cry from the late years of the seventeenth century. The vogue reached its height in 1750 as a fashion for the wealthy and a pastime for the dilettanti, and disturbed the steady growth of national spirit in art. There was a Chinese Festival at Drury Lane Theatre in 1755.

Chippendale snatched his fretwork in his brackets and the angles of his chairs from the Chinese worker in ebony. He erected pagoda-like structures on his cabinets. The Bow china factory termed itself "New Canton," Worcester copied Chinese models, Bristol carried on the story. Staffordshire with her earthenware brought out the "willow-pattern," and a hundred other designs were acclimatized as reflections of the blue and white Canton porcelain.

"Taste is at present the darling idol of the polite world and the world of letters, and, indeed, seems to be considered as the quintessence of almost all the arts and sciences. The fine ladies and gentlemen dress with taste, the architects, whether Gothic or Chinese, build with taste." So writes the essayist in the *Connoisseur* journal in 1756, and he continues ironically, "Whoever makes a pagoda of his parlour fits up his house entirely in taste."

This "Chinese taste" had seized France and Hol-

## THE PERIOD OF LACQUER 109

land. The French artist-craftsmen readily saw that the great influx of Chinese and Japanese furniture would stifle their national artistic impulses. Louis Quatorze had to issue a decree at the end of the seventeenth century to prohibit the import of Oriental wares. The craze reached England later and developed later. But early in the eighteenth century the cabinet-makers of London petitioned Parliament against the importation of manufactured articles from the East Indies to this country. But nothing much seems to have come of their protest. The East India Company had become too powerful to brook interference with its trade by interested artisans. Thousands of lac panels were brought over in the company's ships, even in spite of the deep-rooted belief that lacquer work had at that time become an English art. It is to be presumed that some of the contentions of the old European lacquer-workers may be said to be parallel with the assertions of old potters who asseverated that they had discovered the true porcelain of China. In 1709 Bottger, at Meissen, had for the first time succeeded in producing white hard, paste porcelain, not in imitation of the Chinese, but actually a reproduction of the Oriental technique. But the secret was well kept, and Bottger and his workmen were imprisoned in a fortress. Since Father Du Halde, the Jesuit, had published in Paris in 1725 his *Description de l'Empire de la Chine*, other European potters had endeavoured to find the natural earths of the Chinese, kaolin and petuntse. When William Cookworthy, the chemist and potter of Plymouth, wrote of his discovery of the china clays, Josiah Wedgwood journeyed to Cornwall on a wild-goose chase.

It may be imagined, with data such as these to guide us—first, the growing intensity of the "Chinese taste"; second, the demand for furniture and porcelain on the part of the wealthy classes—that as a consequence an attempt was made to supply the demand.

There were various sources of supply for lacquered furniture, especially lacquered clock-cases. There was the Dutch market, from which was obtained, as in the case of marquetry, panels of lacquered work. At first, without doubt, these came from the East through Holland. The next stage was the Dutch lacquered panel actually produced in Holland. Later there was again the Oriental panel coming straight from the East through our own East India Company. Contemporaneously with these importations, which served as models, there was the lacquered work produced in this country. We shall later attempt to differentiate between these styles.

**Colour versus Form.**—In various epochs the struggle has gone on in the applied arts in regard to the use and abuse of colour in decoration as an adjunct. In furniture the pendulum has swung to and fro. Colour follows form in the process of evolution. In England there is the oak period and the walnut period, where the beauty is solely dependent upon form. The conception of the cabinet-maker has usually been confined to form, eschewing colour, or to colour more or less ignoring the beauty of form, or as a com-

## THE PERIOD OF LACQUER 111

promise, when form has been subservient to colour. When form and colour are in exact harmony the highest ideals are reached in furniture. The Chinese have reached these ideals. The Italian school of the fifteenth century in the marriage coffer, where painting or coloured intarsia is of parallel beauty with the rich carving, achieved like success. With similar judgment, in holding the balance evenly between form and colour, André Charles Boulle conceived his wonderful work in tortoiseshell and brass and ebony and silver, forming a brilliant marquetry of colour, the colour effect being further heightened with a reddish-brown and sometimes a bluish-green ground beneath the semi-transparent tortoiseshell. Riesener and David Roentgen, in equally masterful technique, produced marquetry of tulip-wood, holly, rosewood, purple wood, and laburnum. With the style embodying the enrichment of the plain surface with colour came the use, and later the abuse, of lacquered panels.

A Dutch cabinet-maker, Huygens, had won renown by reproducing remarkable imitations of the Japanese lacquered panel. In Holland, Chinese prototypes had served as models for delft ware. The Dutch potter had simulated the appearance of blue and white Chinese porcelain, but his results were obtained by a white enamel covering a brown body. Dutch lacquer work is similarly imitative of the results rather than a duplication of the Oriental processes. Chintzes and printed "callicoes" equally are surprising efforts at simulation, if not dissimulation.

As a supreme effort of the successful attempt of

the European to reproduce the wonderful limpid transparency of the old Chinese and Japanese work, the secret of Sieur Simon Etienne Martin, a French carriage painter, stands supreme. His varnish, called after him *Vernis-Martin*, has become the term, as in the case of Boulle, for a certain class of technique. In 1744 he obtained the monopoly in France for the manufacture of lacquered work in the Oriental style. He obtained the ground of wavy golden network, such as in rare Japanese panels, and on this Boucher and other artists painted Arcadian subjects.

In England it cannot be said that these great foreign styles have been emulated in the grand manner or even attempted. When colour came to England it came straight from Holland, and *le style réfugié* is responsible for the intermingling of the Dutch and French styles, though the former were at first greatly predominant. The important bureaus and splendid lacquered cabinets produced in the period when colour was employed so lavishly as to disregard form, are attributable, not for the least part of their excellent technique in the skilful employment of lacquer, to the great number of French and other foreign workmen who had settled in this country.

**Peculiarities of the Lacquered Clock-case.**—The use of the lacquered panel in the long case of the clock cannot be said to have a definite period of its own. We cannot mark an exact date when marquetry panels or marquetry " all-over " cases were no longer the vogue, and when lacquered cases succeeded them. The two styles were comparatively contem-

## THE PERIOD OF LACQUER 113

poraneous. Marquetry cases, as we have seen, are as early as 1680, and they continued till about 1725, and later in the provinces. The lacquered case may be said to have run its day from about 1700 to 1755. On the whole they seemed to have had a longer vogue, mainly on account of the prevalence of the " Chinese taste," which demanded colour. Lacquered decoration jumped the experimental stage of reserves or panels that apparently were not quite in exact proportions to the case, but had to be fitted in and sometimes trimmed. It came at a juncture when this difficulty had been mastered. Accordingly, we find the whole of the lacquered case has been regarded as a rectangular surface to be decorated, and we have not met with any instance of more than one lacquered panel being employed on the case. The marquetry case offered other features which indicated the struggle of colour for supremacy. In the early marquetry specimens the turned walnut pillars of the hood belong to an earlier style. They indicate that that form had not been completely ousted. The marquetry worker in the end overcame this and drove these pillars out. In the lacquered case no such struggle is visible. The case is entirely a scheme in colour. It is red, or green, it is black and gold, but the design is never so strong as to tempt one to examine its form. It is simply decorative, but much in the manner that, in textile art, tapestry is pleasing, not challenging a critical examination of form, but suggesting a somnolent restfulness.

Touches of incongruity appear in later examples

of the lacquered clock-case when the arched hood came into fashion and the panel followed suit. It is a shape unsuited to an Oriental design. Such a Western architectural style used in combination with so Eastern a technique as lacquered work is like putting a Corinthian pillar on a Japanese bronze.

The lacquered cases illustrated in this chapter indicate the style. The example with the movement by Joseph Dudds (1766–82), (illustrated p. 115), shows the early attempt to simulate the Eastern style. It is poor and thin, and has not stood the ravages of time and a damp climate.

The specimen (illustrated p. 117), with the movement by Kenneth Maclellan (1760–80), is of more grandiose character. The panelled door was probably an importation, and the other decorations in lacquer done in this country.

Among the Scottish clocks, the Patrick Gordon example (1705–15), (illustrated p. 263), proves this usage of imported Oriental panel with added decoration in as near a style as could be done on the spot. In this example the remainder of the so-called lacquered decoration is stencilled.

**The English School.**—Dutch lacquered work was as prevalent between 1680 and 1725 as was Dutch marquetry. The rivalry between "John Company" and the Dutch traders was one factor that has to be considered. Lacquered work was coming straight from the East to Amsterdam and to English ports. What was not absorbed by the Dutch burghers came to England. Apart from this competitive Oriental trade, there was the lacquered work actually made

LONG-CASE CLOCK WITH LACQUER
DECORATION.

Brass dial with circular medallion with maker's
name, "Joseph Dudds, London" (1766-82).

LONG-CASE CLOCK.

Maker, Kenneth Maclennan (London).
Finely decorated in green lacquer.
Date, 1760–80.
Height, 8 ft.  Width, 1 ft. 8 in.
Depth, 10 in.

(*By courtesy of Percy Webster, Esq.*)

## THE PERIOD OF LACQUER 119

in Holland. In examining the state of that country at this time one meets with a surprise. It was a land teeming with colour. Dutch painters have taught us to think otherwise. The Rijks Museum exhibits the prevalent styles of the seventeenth century. Here we find leather decorations derivative from Spain in rich gilding, Louis Quatorze boudoirs with classic gods and goddesses. The "Chinese Boudoir" from the palace of the Stadtholder at Leeuwarden shows the intense love of colour that had conquered Holland in the late seventeenth century. Here we find the Chinese prototypes in porcelain which provided the potters at Delft with problems to solve, and lacquered work which suggested patient imitation by Dutch cabinet-makers, but the colour and advanced technique of such Oriental originals must have confounded the old craftsmen.

The potter simulated the porcelain with his enamelled earthenware, the cabinet-maker produced lacquered work which passed muster in Holland and England. Take the house of the rich burgher. The table was covered with an Eastern rug, called a "table carpet." The linen cupboards so beloved by the Dutch were surmounted by Chinese and Japanese porcelain. Often a Japanese lac cabinet gave another touch of colour to the interior. Rich damask curtains, Spanish leather hangings, Oriental rugs, finely inlaid cabinets of ebony and silver, and a glowing array of copper and brass, filled the heart of the Dutch *vrouw* with pride. Such rooms were regarded as a "holy of holies," and the family had their meals in the kitchen or living room and were warned off the show room. The seventeenth-century Dutchwoman, according to all accounts, seems to have been a shrew. But enough is extant to prove that Holland was artistically, in regard to the home-life of Stadtholder and burgher, resplendent with colour, in spite of the low tones of the canvases of Dutch painters.

In England, too, the love of colour was becoming predominant. Fifty thousand Huguenot families, with their Latin blood and love of colour, scattered in the Protestant countries had no inconsiderable influence. Spitalfields silk is as English as the dark and tortuous lanes from which it emanates. But every weaver had a French name, and although the industry has come to an end, to-morrow, if the demand arose, the descendants of these French Huguenots would again stand at the looms to produce English silk.

The sudden outburst of colour in the now rarely prized English lacquered cabinets and bureaus must be attributed to the foreign workmen in our midst at the close of the seventeenth century. It is English perforce, because it was made in England. The followers of Huygens the Dutchman and the disciples of Martin the Frenchman were capable of producing something new and something surprising in English cabinet work. The foreign quarters of London have always been the centre of art industry. Armenians sit on the roofs of fashionable West End emporiums and restore carpets and rugs. Polish and Russian furriers travel by the

# THE PERIOD OF LACQUER 121

Tube from Whitechapel and Bethnal Green, from the Commercial Road and Shoreditch to Regent Street and Bond Street with their handiwork. What is now, was two hundred and fifty years ago. Alien craftsmen, more skilled than the English workmen, worked for less wages and produced better work.

The English style, therefore, of the late seventeenth century in lacquered work was as English as the work of Daniel Marot the Frenchman and of Grinling Gibbons the Dutch woodcarver at Hampton Court.

The English style is praised as something fine and original as a European replica of the Oriental. So it is. It is the French grafted on to the Dutch and acclimatized here. It holds the same place in lacquered work as the Dutch delft ware does in ceramics. It is a splendid imitation of a technique not grasped by the imitator. Lovers of lacquered rarities and collectors of the so-called English style, so rare and so much extolled, can take it to heart that it is really English—as English as the canvases of Vandyck or the painted panels of ergolesi.

**English Amateur Imitators.**—There are records enough to show that the art of lacquer had appealed to the amateur on account of its apparent simplicity. It is ludicrous to read of the attempts of seventeenth-century teachers of the art of "japanning" to young ladies. The seventeenth-century "miss," according to old memoirs, left her Stuart stump needlework, with its quaint costume and crude figures, to simulate the subtle art of the Chinese or Japanese lacquer-worker. At that time the greatest coach-panel painter could not have approached the finesse of the lacquered work coming from the East. In spite of Stalker and Parker in 1688, with their treatise how to produce lacquered "japanning" in the Oriental style—a guide for amateurs and the standard work for all the academies that taught this new accomplishment—we cannot believe much of this amateur work found its way on clock-cases, which in point of time heralded the oncoming burst of colour. It is incredible that all of a sudden, following the clock-case and the chair-back, fine red and green and black and gold lac decoration, as exhibited by rich cabinets and gorgeous bureaus scintillating with colour, could have succeeded the stump-work amateurs. Stalker and company must go by the board as caterers for a very amateur taste. Their book possibly never reached the trade, or if it did, it could have had very little influence upon adept refugees practising a subtle art.

**Painted Furniture not Lacquered Work.**—Whatever may be determined as to the merits of *Vernis-Martin* or of the creations of Huygens the Dutchman in regard to comparison with Chinese and Japanese prototypes, it is certain that English amateur work, which is often dull gold design on a black ground, is not only an echo but a feeble echo of the original. They are splendid examples of dulness. Pepys complains that women wore feathers in his day. The feminine instinct is difficult to reckon with. Some years ago very up-to-date young wives "aspinalled" everything pea-green or peacock-blue. They did a lot of damage. Similarly, in the seventeenth century, when the boudoir escaped from needlework into lacquer, much otherwise harmless furniture must have been spoilt. Hundreds of fine pieces of furniture were brought up to date by the simple process of painting them and simulating the Chinese lacquered work. In the Early Victorian age of graining, sapient workmen painted solid oak panels and grained them to resemble the oak that they had painted. Folly is not the monopoly of any age. It is eternal. To-day the framer, if he is not watched and carefully instructed, glues a fine engraving to a sheet of cardboard and rubs a wet cloth over the surface of the print, destroying its beauty for ever with his clod-like smudge. Fools are ever present to confound the conservation of art treasures.

Painting a surface, however Oriental it may be in design, is *not* lacquer work. Half the so-called lacquered work is merely painting with a coat of varnish put on it. When Sheraton and his school brought French painted panels into fashion in this country, they brought a true art. But it was not lacquer. Cipriani, Angelica Kauffmann, and Pergolesi, who used their brushes on cabinet work, and Zoffany, who did not disdain to paint clock-cases for Rimbault, brought a new style to this country. It was the age of colour-prints in the French taste; the Wards, the George Morlands, and the Bartolozzis demanded colour as a suitable environment. Satinwood and coloured marquetry and the painted panel accordingly found a place at this moment.

The amateur attempts of the late seventeenth

and eighteenth centuries, up to the *furore* of the "Chinese taste" in 1750, must be disregarded as something outside the field of the collector—that is, if he is desirous of selecting lacquered work of excellent character. As a phase of fashionable caprice it is no doubt interesting, but it is to be hoped that most of these amateur efforts have succumbed to the influence of time and have been destroyed. They represent nothing in particular except a sham imitation of a great art, as stupidly offensive as was Strawberry Hill, the Gothic toy of Horace Walpole.

**The Inn Clock.**—We interpolate here a short outline of a class of clocks which appeals to collectors. In America they are termed "banjo clocks." A good deal has been written about them, connecting them with Pitt's tax on clocks and watches in 1797 of five shillings on each clock per annum, which Act was repealed in the next year. It is supposed that these clocks suddenly came into being when private clocks were taxed, and were used in inns. Owing to such a deep-seated belief they are always known throughout the country as "Act of Parliament" clocks. But they were used earlier than the Act of 1797, and were probably ordinary inn clocks in common use about that time. They were wall clocks varnished with black lacquer, mostly plain, but sometimes decorated in gold. Often the figures were in white and they had no protective glass.

The example illustrated (p. 125) is decorated in black and gold lacquer, and the name on the dial is John Grant, Fleet Street, about 1785. This is

INN CLOCK.

Decorated in black and gold lacquer.
Maker, John Grant (Fleet Street). About 1785.
Formerly in possession of Sir Augustus Harris.

(*By courtesy of John R. Southworth, Esq.*)

## THE PERIOD OF LACQUER

rather an elaborate specimen, as most of the ordinary inn clocks of this shape are innocent of these rather elaborate lacquer enrichments. They are to be found all over the country; we have seen one in an inn at Evesham. They are in Kent and the south, but do not appear to have been in common use in the northern counties, unless imported there later. Ale-house jests are frequent on old earthenware mugs—" Drink faire, don't swear "—and broad hints as to credit. This is similarly found as a standing pointed jest in an "Act of Parliament" clock in a Kentish inn, minus the works, with the inscription "No Tick "—a jest which the most seasoned toper could readily understand.

Oliver Goldsmith, when he wrote his *Deserted Village* in 1770, is said to have described in "Sweet Auburn" a typical Irish village in regard to its desertion, but he introduced touches reminiscent of his town habits. When he wrote of the village alehouse :—

> The whitewash'd wall, the nicely sanded floor,
> The varnish'd clock that click'd behind the door,

he may have been thinking of inn clocks he had seen in Fleet Street. By his use of the word "varnished" it would appear that Goldsmith had in mind the ale-house clock of which we are speaking. There was no other that was "varnished," that is, lacquered. The term "Act of Parliament" clocks must therefore be discarded; these clocks were common inn clocks, and had nothing to do with the Act levying the tax in 1797.

As a rule, elaborately lacquered examples of such clocks should be regarded with caution by the collector. The inn clock was "varnished," but it had no panelled lacquer and lattice-work gold ornament. It was a simple hanging wall clock *sans* artistic embellishment.

# CHAPTER V

# THE LONG-CASE CLOCK
# THE GEORGIAN PERIOD

## CHAPTER V

THE LONG-CASE CLOCK—THE GEORGIAN PERIOD

The stability of the "grandfather" clock—The burr-walnut period — Thomas Chippendale — The mahogany period—Innovations of form—The Sheraton style—Marquetry again employed in decoration.

To collectors and connoisseurs the most desirable period of the long-case clock is from 1700 to about 1720. As we have seen in the previous chapters, this embraces the two styles of marquetry and lacquered work, although lacquered work continued to the middle of the eighteenth century. The year 1720 is not an arbitrary date, but this year is a convenient one. It marks the accession of the first of the Four Georges and the advent of the House of Hanover. As the title to a period of time, the Georgian period is as good as any other. Just a hundred years afterwards George III died, and the Fourth George reigned only ten years, till 1830.

In regard to the clock-case, the century was not filled with great changes. The writers of memoirs of the time—Selwyn and Walpole, Lord Hervey and

Fanny Burney—furnish many sidelights on the Georgian period. Thackeray in his *Four Georges* illuminated the Georgian era with more vigour than Early Victorians could stand. The eighteenth century is repellent by its stupidity and coarseness, by its insipidity and dulness, and yet it is relieved by a continuity of extraordinary forcefulness and freshness of vigour, undimmed in our naval and military history, unequalled in our art and letters. The following names occur to prove this suggestion: Clive and Warren Hastings, Rodney and Nelson, Moore and Wellington, Reynolds and Gainsborough, Dr. Johnson and Burke.

We lost, but not for ever, the love of the American Colonies for the great Mother Country, whose tongue is a common heritage, and whose democratic freedom is akin to that across the Atlantic, and this through the obstinacy of a German monarch thwarting the will of the people. "The first and second Georges were not Englishmen, and therefore were not popular, and excited no enthusiasm in their subjects, but were simply tolerated as being better than the Popish Stuarts"; so says Lord Macaulay in his *Essay on Chatham*. It is ludicrous to learn that Walpole, beefy Englishman that he was, spoke no French, and had, as George I spoke no English, to conduct State affairs in Latin. What a stratum of misunderstanding on which to rest a people's destinies!

**The Stability of the "Grandfather" Clock.**—The long-case clock had become a piece of furniture. It was of marquetry decoration, in keeping with con-

LONG-CASE CLOCK.

Maker, Henderson (London).
Date, about 1770.
Height, 9 ft.   Width, 1 ft. 8½ in.
Depth, 11 in.

## THE GEORGIAN PERIOD

temporary tables and cabinets, or it was lacquered in rich colours in "Chinese taste" to keep touch with the Oriental parlours. But concurrent with the age of marquetry and lacquer was the great walnut period. The delightful veneer of burr-walnut in Queen Anne days in cabinets and chests of drawers and other important pieces of furniture did not neglect the clock-case. The gnarled figure of the walnut was essentially a proper decoration to apply to the clock-case.

The long-case clock had not only become acclimatized, but it had become thoroughly English. The simplicity of its construction, and its proud record as a perfect timekeeper, gave it the supremacy over all other clocks. English clockmakers, with the fine sense of practical utility which governed their employment of mechanism, had reached a point when further inventions became more of scientific use than popular. The "grandfather" clock has no equal within its limits. It runs for eight days. Its construction is so simple that when needing repair it need not be sent to a specialist. It has no delicate parts to confound the provincial maker. Hence it has lasted two centuries and more as a standard English clock. There is, too, a certain lovableness about the "grandfather" clock. The popular term suggests this. It is the heritage of the poor. The "grandfather" clock of the yeomanry has passed down through many generations. Indeed, the love of it as an article of furniture has, in many instances, endowed it with a value far greater than it possesses.

**The Burr-walnut Period.**—Veneer had become an established technique. Woods with fine figure served as panels laid on wood of lesser rarity or decorative importance. Oak was a good foundation for walnut veneer. Earlier, as we have seen, walnut was laid as a ground on oak and the marquetry design laid on the walnut. But in the burr-walnut period carefully selected walnut sheets were employed to decorate surfaces of bureaus and clock-cases. The age of walnut is synonymous with the days of Hogarth.

Burr-walnut clock-cases are not so frequently found as could be wished. The burr-walnut panels are marked in a series of knot-like rings, obtained from the gnarled roots of the walnut-tree. The peculiar pleasing effect of this and other mottled walnut is heightened by the mellow effect time always gives to these walnut examples, which cannot be produced with any appreciable success by modern imitators.

**Thomas Chippendale—The Mahogany Period.**—There is no doubt that the name of Thomas Chippendale will always be representative of the mahogany period of English furniture. But there were other makers contemporary with him who did splendid work. The Chippendales, Thomas the father and Thomas the son, picture-frame carver and cabinet-maker at Worcester, migrated together to London in 1729. The son, Thomas, published his *Director* in 1754. He was the leading cabinet-maker and designer of his day, and his day lasted till about 1780, when his son, Thomas Chippendale the third entered

LONG-CASE CLOCK.

Maker, Thomas Wagstaff (Gracechurch Street, London). Date, about 1780. Height, 8 ft. 2 in. Width, 1 ft. 7½ in. Depth, 10 in.

*(By courtesy of Percy Webster, Esq.)*

LONG-CASE CLOCK.

Movement by Stephen Rimbault, case by Robert Adam.
Date, about 1775.

(*By courtesy of Messrs. A. B. Daniell & Sons.*)

## THE GEORGIAN PERIOD 141

into partnership with Haig, and the firm became Chippendale and Haig, who also in turn produced magnificent work. Close upon the heels of the Chippendales was the firm of Hepplewhite. The brothers Adam, architectural designers and creators of furniture suitable for its new classic environment, began to make their impress upon interior decoration and on furniture, as they had upon Princes Street, Edinburgh, the Quays at Dublin, and the Adelphi in London, with their patent stucco mouldings and festoons.

Accordingly, the student must bear in mind these great movements taking place during the second half of our Georgian period, viz. from about 1740 to the year 1791, at which date appeared the first edition of Sheraton's *Cabinet Maker and Upholsterer's Drawing Book*, to herald another style, blended with the Adam, but departing from it at important points. In examining clock-cases of this prolific and restless period, it should be of exceptional interest to the connoisseur to show how unnamed cabinet-makers in London and in the provinces attempted to employ, with varying degrees of skill, the designs promulgated broadcast by these great teachers of design and construction in cabinet work.

**Innovations of Form.**—As exemplifying the variations of the mahogany period clock-case, we illustrate several types showing reflections of the great impulses that were in the air. The clock, illustrated (p. 239), has a case of Spanish mahogany with fine figure. The hood is enriched with fretwork, and with elegantly moulded door, and the superstructure as a pediment exhibits the Chinese style. The terminals are mahogany. The dial shows phases of the moon, and the movement is by a provincial maker, E. Cockey, Warminster.

Of the year 1770 is another mahogany clock with handsomely carved frieze and elaborate terminals. The love for architectural ornament is seen in the hood, and in the pillars on the waist below on each side of the panelled door. The base is decorated with a panel, in mahogany of fine figure. The feet are beginning to become more pronounced. The movement of this is by Henderson, of London, and its height is 9 feet (illustrated p. 133).

Another clock, by Thomas Wagstaff, in date about 1780, exhibits a less grandiose appearance. The height is less, being only 8 feet 2 inches. The pediment of the hood reverts to types which are often found decorated with lacquer work, and the brass terminals are of similar character to those of an earlier period. It is noticeable that the base continues to show increased ornament in the feet, with an added scroll (illustrated p. 137).

As showing another type of clock with magnificent decoration we illustrate (p. 143) the hood of a long-case musical clock, attributed to Rimbault, who was especially noteworthy for his musical movements, and his cases were decorated by Zoffany. An examination of this shows the detailed character of the painted work. It is Italian in conception, and quite in keeping with other work of Zoffany.

Another illustration (p. 139) shows the typical classical style. The case was designed by Robert

TOP PORTION OF MUSICAL LONG-CASE CLOCK.

Richly decorated with painting attributed to Zoffany.
Maker, no signature, but suggestive of the work of Rimbault.

(*By courtesy of Messrs. Harris & Sinclair, Dublin.*)

LONG-CASE CLOCK.

Eight-day movement. Mahogany case inlaid with satinwood shell designs and banding.
Maker, James Hatton, London (1800-12).
Brick design in base in Chippendale manner.

(*By courtesy of Messrs. D. Sherratt & Co., Chester.*)

## THE GEORGIAN PERIOD 147

Adam, and is in date about 1775. The dial becomes circular, and owes certain of its decoration to French form, although it is surmounted by a Greek urn, but the flying garlands betray it. The waist becomes tapered, terminating in a base of graceful proportions and reticent ornament. The fluted work and the scroll indicate the design of the architect. One can imagine such a chaste clock finding itself in the cold, un-English environment of Ken Wood, or on the staircase of some learned society, with candelabra of bronze of classic design, with hoofs as feet and with the Roman lamp throwing out its modern flame. The movement of this clock is by Stephen Rimbault, of Great St. Andrew Street, about 1775.

Another example of a clock by James Hatton, London (about 1810), exhibits several new features. Its case is of rich feathered mahogany, inlaid in the Sheraton manner with satinwood shells, banding, and herring-bone stringing. The hood is massive and reverts to an earlier period, and the ornament of the base, in brickwork style, was known to have been employed by Chippendale. The finials are brass. The dial is brass, and in the lunette are painted a ship and a cottage (illustrated p. 145).

For the continuation of these styles one must turn to the provincial makers (Chapter VIII), showing a variety of decoration and touches of incongruity in style and anachronism in date—a glorious intermingling of contemporary with bygone features, affording unequalled delight to the collector. In the case of provincial made furniture, whole districts carried on fashions for a quarter of a century or longer after they had been forgotten in London, and the clock-case is no exception.

Included in this period is the fine clock (illustrated p. 149) by Robert Molyneux and Sons, London, 1825, now in the Bristol Museum. It has one main dial recording minutes, and two smaller dials showing hours and seconds respectively. The main dial has two hands, which indicate Greenwich mean time and Bristol time. The type is known as a "regulator" clock, with the twenty-four-hour dial and other additions appertaining to the astronomical clock. The illustration shows the time to be: Greenwich, 11.42 (i.e. 42 minutes past 11 o'clock); Bristol, 11.32 (i.e. 10 minutes difference). The clock has a mercury pendulum. There was a somewhat similar clock constructed by Dell, of Bristol.

LONG-CASE REGULATOR CLOCK.

Movement by Robert Molyneux & Sons, London, 1825. Three dials, one showing hours and one seconds, the great dial showing Greenwich time and Bristol time.

ENLARGEMENT OF DIAL.

The two hands on large or minute dial show difference of 10 minutes 22 seconds between Greenwich and Bristol time.

(*By permission of Bristol Museum and Art Gallery.*)

# CHAPTER VI

# THE EVOLUTION OF THE LONG-CASE CLOCK

## CHAPTER VI

### THE EVOLUTION OF THE LONG-CASE CLOCK

Its inception—Its Dutch origin—The changing forms of the hood, the waist, and the base—The dial and its character—The ornamentation of the spandrel—The evolution of the hands.

FROM 1680 to 1850 is a long period of time for a particular style of timepiece to run without interruption or without displacement by any other fashion. It may naturally be supposed that during this period changes have occurred in form, in decoration, and in a score of minor details delightful to the collector and interesting to the student of form in design. The inception of the long case was due to the common use of the seconds pendulum. This required a certain space to swing in, and the pendulum was of a certain length. This undue length does not seem to have been necessary in the wall clock of the so-called "Act of Parliament" type, and as Lord Grimthorpe, the constructor of "Big Ben" at Westminster, says: "Spring clocks are generally resorted to for the purpose of saving length; for as clocks are generally made in England, it is impossible to make a weight clock capable of going a week, without either a case nearly 4 feet high, or else the weights so heavy as to produce a great friction on the arbour of the great wheel. But this arises from nothing but the heaviness of the wheels and the badness of the pinions used in most English clocks, as is amply proved by the fact that the American and Austrian clocks go a week with smaller weights and much less fall than English ones, and the American ones with no assistance from fine workmanship for the purpose of diminishing friction, as they are remarkable for their want of what is called 'finish' in the machinery, on which so much time and money is wasted in English clock-work."

**Its Dutch Origin.**—As we have before explained, the marquetry case came straight from Holland. Our "grandfather" was a Dutchman, as far as clock-cases go. The Dutchman Huygens is credited with having been the first to employ the pendulum in the mechanism of the clock. Leonardo da Vinci, that stupendous genius, left notes as to his study of the pendulum (1452–1520), and Galileo came with his later studies (1564–1642). It is a disputed point as to when and where the pendulum came into being. We must accept Huygens (1629–95) as the practical exponent of the pendulum, although not the original discoverer of its properties. But at any rate, the long-case clock may be generally accepted as coincident with the use of the long or seconds pendulum. And to Holland we must look for this habitual usage of the long wooden case to protect the weights and the pendulum.

# EVOLUTION OF LONG-CASE CLOCK

Among the designs of Marot there are drawings of long-case clocks certainly more ornate than those usually associated with such an early period (this was about 1660 to 1680), and French Louis XIV and Louis XV tall clocks are built on these lines, and Chippendale at a later period found Marot an exceedingly prolific master of design to study.

**The Changing Forms of the Hood, the Waist, and the Base.**—The evolution of form in one class of object from one period to another is of exceptional interest. In furniture, in china, in glass, and in silver, the progression of forms is so marked as to give practically a date to each piece. The gate-leg table can be traced from three to twelve legs with double gates. The chair, from its straight oaken back and massive arms to the tapering legs and curves of the satinwood period, runs through stages as definitely marked as though the makers had signed the pieces. Now the stretcher is low, next it becomes higher, then it disappears altogether; or the splats in the back are single, then double, with cane panels, and then again upholstered. The top rail of the chair affords similar delectation to the connoisseur of form changing for a definite reason.

The clock-case underwent equal changes in character, not only in its decoration, as we have seen, in marquetry, in lacquer, and in veneers of burr-walnut and mahogany, but its proportions varied. At first, coming as it did in the walnut period, the hood had turned rails, in keeping with the turned rails of the chairs of the time. The hood was square and small, the waist was more slender, and the base in proportion. During the marquetry and the lacquered periods the hood began to grow larger and more dominant. It had a domed superstructure, and the finials or metal terminals were more ornamental and grew in number (see illustrations, pp. 133, 117). The massive character of the early mahogany period, culminating with Chippendale, had its effect on the long clock-case. The hood had a pagoda-like edifice in the Chinese style (see illustration, p. 239), or it had the woodcarver's adoption of architecture, as in the crest of the hood (see illustrations, pp. 145, 117). The rail in the hood had become a Corinthian pillar, and later a pilaster. At the end of the eighteenth and beginning of the nineteenth century it had a new form: when it was turned mahogany it stood away from the case, as an ornament apart, rather than a supporting pillar (see illustration, p. 233). This is a noticeable feature in country-made clocks of this period.

At first there was no door in the case. But on the introduction of the door, its panelled form commenced to make its progression in form in accompaniment with the other features of the case. It was square, in simple forms, with square hoods. In 1730 it took the form somewhat similar to the shape of the lowest marquetry panel, as shown in the clock by Jas. Leicester (see Frontispiece). It really follows the chair-backs of a period of some ten or fifteen years' prior date. It is an instance of the clock-case slightly lagging behind contemporary furniture design. The shapes of these panels re-

# EVOLUTION OF LONG-CASE CLOCK

semble the chair-backs of the James II, William and Mary, and the Queen Anne period. In some instances the simple form becomes taller, terminating in a small semicircle. The Sussex iron fire-backs of the seventeenth century show similar forms of panel.

By 1770 the panel had lost its lunette or semi-circular form at top, and in outline resembled a Chippendale chair-back. The evolution is easily traceable. A similar fashion is observed in tombstones in old country churchyards. By the late eighteenth and early nineteenth centuries, especially in certain North of England type clock-cases, notably Lancashire and Cheshire, these panels are Gothic in character (see illustration, p. 231). Following French fashion, in some late examples there is a glass panel (see illustration, p. 275).

The base undergoes certain changes, though in a lesser degree. Sometimes plain, sometimes with a plinth, sometimes with feet. Dutch long clock-cases have great wooden balls as feet. In the Chippendale period the plinth has a suggestion of Chinese character. In later types the feet are more pronounced, and the base has an ornamental panel in the Sheraton period with a delicate marquetry inlay of simple character. In Sheraton's *Design Book* there are two clocks showing the base further ornamented by turned pillars similar to the hood.

The growing importance of these feet and their frequent use, especially in ornate examples, are shown in the specimens illustrated (pp. 133, 137).

**The Dial and its Character.**—When only one hand was in use, it was obviously not necessary to denote the minutes. Later, the minutes were engraved on the dial to meet the use of the minute hand; sometimes these were in a circle inside the hour numerals, and later they were put on the outer edge, outside the hour numerals. The hour numerals are almost invariably of Roman style, and the figure IV has by universal custom been engraved IIII, though there are examples of a late period with IV which are of country make. Similarly, Arabic figures have also been used. The illustration of a fine dial, of eighteenth century period, showing the various phases of the iron industry at Ashburnham, in Sussex, has these figures; this is a country-made clock (p. 243).

The dials were brass, and the hour numerals appeared on a circle of brass plated with silver. Iron dials were used later, in the decadent period, and both numerals and floral designs were painted on the enamelled surface in lieu of engraved and ornamental metal-work, and often a landscape or figure subject occupied the lunette.

The lunette form followed the square face, and sometimes the maker put his name in this lunette, and later below the centre of the clock, and later again not at all on the dial. The lunette form no doubt determined the shape of the panel of the door in the case below, to which we have previously alluded. The illustration (p. 159) shows these forms. The dial, by Henry Massy (1680), has the name between the numerals VI and VII. The lunette form in a dial by John Draper (1703) has

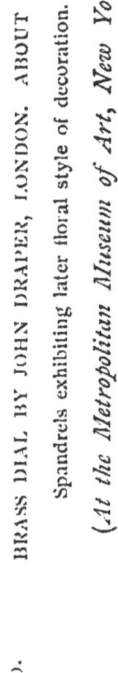

BRASS DIAL BY JOHN DRAPER, LONDON. ABOUT 1703.
Spandrels exhibiting later floral style of decoration.
(At the Metropolitan Museum of Art, New York.)

BRASS DIAL BY HENRY MASSY, LONDON. ABOUT 1680.
Clock with usual eight-day movement.
(An enlargement of this dial is illustrated p. 163.)
(By courtesy of Edward Campbell, Esq., Glasgow.)

# EVOLUTION OF LONG-CASE CLOCK

the name of the maker in a circular disc above the hour circle.

Enlargements of the Henry Massy dial and of another by John Bushman show the character of engraving and the position of the maker's name (illustrated p. 163).

In regard to the engraving put on the dials of these old clocks, it is not impossible that William Hogarth, when he was an apprentice at Master Ellis Gamble's shop, at the sign of the "Golden Angel" in Cranbourn Street, Leicester Fields, did some of this work. We know that Thomas Bewick engraved clock dials when an apprentice at Newcastle-upon-Tyne (see p. 215).

The last form of the long-case dial is circular, an unusual type in vogue during the closing decades of the eighteenth century, belonging to the classic and French styles and in no way diverting the fashion of the main stream of case-makers.

Concerning the use of glass for the protection of the dial in the long-case clock, it was in use in coaches for the first time in 1667. According to Pepys' *Diary* we learn : " Another pretty thing was my Lady Ashly's speaking of the bad qualities of the glass coaches, among others the flying open of the doors upon any great shake ; but another, my Lady Peterborough, being in her glass coach with the glass up, and seeing a lady pass by in a coach whom she would salute, the glass was so clear that she thought it had been open, and so ran her head through the glass."

At first the hood of the clock lifted off and the

glass was fixed; later the glass was framed in a door, and subsequently the hood slid off, which fashion is found in all but the earliest examples.

The term "dial" is a survival of the word "sundial." Like all innovations, there may have been those who preferred the old character, or it may have been left to Charles Lamb, lover of past and faded memories, to ruminate on garden gods in the Temple: "What an antique air had the now almost effaced sundials, with their moral inscriptions, seeming coevals with that Time which they measured, and to take their revelations of its flight immediately from heaven, holding correspondence with the fountain of light. . . . The shepherd, 'carved it out quaintly in the sun,' and turning philosopher by the very occupation, provided it with mottoes more touching than tombstones." Elia, Shakespearean scholar that he was, could not have forgotten the melancholy Jaques with his:—

> I met a fool i' the forest,
> A motley fool; a miserable world!
> As I do live by food, I met a fool;
> Who laid him down and bask'd him in the sun,
> And rail'd on Lady Fortune in good terms,
> In good set terms and yet a motley fool.
> "Good morrow, fool," quoth I. "No, sir," quoth he,
> "Call me not fool till heaven hath sent me fortune":
> And then he drew a dial from his poke,
> And, looking on it with lack-lustre eye,
> Says very wisely: "It is ten o'clock:
> Thus we may see," quoth he, "how the world wags:
> 'Tis but an hour ago since it was nine,
> And after one hour more 'twill be eleven;
> And so, from hour to hour, we ripe and ripe,
> And then, from hour to hour, we rot and rot;
> And thereby hangs a tale."

ENLARGEMENT OF DIAL.

Showing maker's name, John Bushman, London. About 1680.
From lantern clock illustrated as Frontispiece.

ENLARGEMENT OF DIAL.

Showing maker's name, Hen. Massy, London, and square dial indicating date of month. About 1680.
From long-case clock illustrated p. 159.

# EVOLUTION OF LONG-CASE CLOCK

It is not probable that the "fool i' the forest" drew from his pocket a sundial; it was, no doubt, a pocket-clock, or, in other words, a watch.

The art of dial-making is a subtle one. It is true that some are pleasing in their balance and others are displeasing, which sets us wondering what rules there are to govern the symmetrical arrangement of circles and figures and their co-related hands. There is an air of solemn grandeur about a fine dial; its dignity is as unruffled as the march of Time itself. The old masters of dial construction had the art of spacing as completely under control as had Caxton the great typographer in the balance of his printed page.

What Lord Grimthorpe has said[1] about the dials of turret clocks applies in its principles to the dials of domestic clocks. "The figures are generally made much too large. People have a pattern dial painted; and if the figures are not as long as one-third of the radius, and therefore occupying, with the minutes, about two-thirds of the area of the dial, they fancy they are not large enough to be read at a distance; whereas the fact is, the more the dial is occupied by figures, the less distinct they are, and the more difficult it is to distinguish the position of the hands, which is what people want to see, and not to read the figures, which may very well be replaced by twelve large spots. . . . The rule which has been adopted, after various experiments, as the best for the proportions of the dial is this: Divide the radius into three, and leave the

[1] *Encyclopædia Britannica* (ninth edition), vol. vi.

inner two-thirds clear and flat, and of some colour forming a strong contrast to the colour of the hands—black or dark blue if they are gilt, and white if they are black. The figures, if there are any, should occupy the next two-thirds of the remaining third, and the minutes be set in the remainder near the edge."

**The Ornamentation of the Spandrel.**—There are some interesting types of ornamentation of the space between the hour circle and the square outlines of the dial. The neat filling of spandrels offered problems to the architect and woodworker long before the clockmaker found similar difficulties. It is not easy exactly to fill a triangle with a design that is pleasing. Some of the best examples are found in Italian lettering, old sixteenth-century woodcuts of the letter L.

In English clocks, the spandrel in the lantern clock about 1670 had a plain cherub head, as simple in character as the fine pearwood carving from a Buckinghamshire church we illustrate of a slightly earlier period, still rich with unimpaired colour (p. 167). German clocks had this device of the cherub's head, but not in the spandrel. At the British Museum there is one example with this cherub-head as a base ornament at the foot of the clock, which rests on it. This is in date 1600.

The design of the cherub with outspread wings was common enough in Italy, where children have served as models since Donatello. It became established as a form and was a favourite embellishment of the English stone-carver in the seventeenth

BRASS SPANDREL.

From dial of clock by Henry Massy (London), 1680, illustrated p. 159.

century. Horace Walpole protested at its abuse by the contemporaries of Christopher Wren, and it can be found outside St. Paul's Cathedral and in many other London churches and over late Stuart doorways.

It was, therefore, nothing new; it was a pleasing spandrel ornament which appealed to the clockmaker as suitable to clock dials. It naturally received floriated additions, and both in its simpler form and in this later and more elaborate variation it appears on the spandrels of clock dials (see p. 167).

It is interesting to find the clockmaker so conservative. Once the cherub found its way on to clocks, there it remained. It is in the clock at Windsor Castle which Henry VIII gave to Anne Boleyn, formerly at Strawberry Hill before Queen Victoria purchased it. In its first form on the spandrel it practically followed the simple woodcarver's design we illustrate, but with this difference: the triangle to be filled by the clockmaker in his spandrels, at each of the four corners of his dial, was exactly opposite to that of the woodcarver or the stone-carver where he made a bracket. The triangle in these cases stood on its apex. The clockmaker's triangle stood on its base. Hence it will be observed that a straight line drawn along the head of the cherub (p. 167) finds itself level with the top of the two wings. The clockmaker modified this in his metal spandrel ornaments. He dropped the wings, so that the top of the cherub's head is the apex of the triangle and the tips of the two wings the base.

Later, the head, although still retained, was enveloped in floriated ornament and the cherub became unrecognizable. But the triangle is well filled.

We next come to a most interesting stage, coincident in time with the rebuilding of Hampton Court. The "Glorious Revolution" had become established and James II sent packing. The two cherubs holding up the Protestant crown would seem by its prevalence at this period to be a sort of symbolic record of events that were happening. Huguenot and Dutch metal-workers put their thoughts into form, and we find this William and Mary Protestant emblem on the clock-face (see p. 171).

But we also find it on the stretcher of the walnut chair of the period (as illustrated, p. 171). Nor is this all. Lambeth and Bristol delft dishes contribute their pæan in honour of the House of Orange. On some a crown is found, with the date 1690, the sole decoration of a plate some 9 inches in diameter. On others a crown is shown on a cushion, with the sceptre and orb beside it. These are all contemporary with other English delft dishes bearing crudely painted portraits of William and Mary crowned.

Cardinal Wolsey's coat of arms, as shown at Hampton Court, was two cherubs supporting a cardinal's hat. One can imagine that Queen Mary, backed by little Christopher Wren, brought Daniel Marot and Grinling Gibbons to put an end to all this. Accordingly, if one pays a pilgrimage to Hampton Court one sees the carved angels triumphantly holding up the Protestant crown to supplant

BRASS SPANDREL OF DIAL OF CLOCK.
Showing design of angels supporting crown.

Wolsey's former insignia of arrogant splendour under the old religion.

In regard to the long continuance of this design, it is interesting to observe that it appears in plates attributed to the Lowestoft factory. As a matter of fact, such plates were made in Holland to the order of some shipmaster. They usually celebrate the wedding of some persons in the district, whose names are still known. They are decorated in blue, and have two cherubs supporting a heart, over which is a crown. There is one dated 1755, inscribed "Henry and Mary Quinton, Yarmouth, Norfolk." Its Dutch origin is proven by the orthography with the two dots over the letters *y*, and the misplacing of other letters: "Henrÿ and Marÿ Qüinton, Yarmoüth, nor ff: olk. 1755."

After the two cherubs on the clock spandrel came further floriated designs minus the cherub's head. This, later, disappeared, and the spandrel had only a matted surface, in contrast to the rest of the dial. This in turn disappeared when the dial departed from its former glory of a silvered hour circle and became a sheet of iron painted according to taste. We give examples of this—the Sussex dial depicting the iron works (p. 243) and the provincial style with the lunette painted with a figure subject (p. 249). The end of the story is the china dial of the painted Hindeloopen Dutch clocks beloved of our childhood, with weights and chains and other pleasing mechanism. Here the nineteenth-century Dutch clock joins hands with the old wall clock of the seventeenth century, Dame Fashion having pirouetted round the dial, trifling with all collectors in "the whirligig of time."

**The Evolution of the Hands.**—The early examples of the long-case clock or of the lantern clock with one hand show a fine rich design in metal-work in the hand itself. It was brass, often gilded, or iron wrought with great skill and beauty. At the advent of the minute hand it was made in character with its fellow. At first the dial had a *fleur-de-lis*, and later a slightly more floriated use of this emblem on the hour circle between each hour. In old examples the hand, when it came opposite this decoration, was in keeping with the *fleur-de-lis* as though it were part of the design of the hand. It is only a fancy, but, as no design comes by accident, it is very probable that such was the idea of the old dial engraver.

The study of hands is exceptionally interesting; they run through a regular series of styles, as varied as the ornamentation of the cases. Some of the designs are of exquisite balance as specimens of delicate metal-work, in which the English have always been proficient. Their character can be gauged by the expert clockmaker or connoisseur to such a nicety that it can be seen at once if the clock has its original hands or not. Those of my readers who wish to pursue this subject will find the hands adequately treated and well illustrated in *English Domestic Clocks*, by Mr. Herbert Cesinsky and Mr. Malcolm R. Webster, a volume which no student of clocks should fail to consult as a practical and authoritative work.

# EVOLUTION OF LONG-CASE CLOCK

In regard to hands, it is curious that the fashion of placing a minute hand to travel around the dial with the hour hand has established a method of reckoning time in a popular manner not in accordance with scientific exactitude. The eye glances at the dial and sees that the minute hand has so many minutes to travel *before* reaching the next hour. We accordingly say, for instance, it is twenty minutes to four or ten minutes to four. On one half of the dial we have acted quite scientifically in saying it is ten minutes past three or half-past three, but the moment the point of the half hour is reached we act in a different manner. We never speak or think of four thirty-five, four forty, or four fifty, unless we have to consult the railway time-table.

This all comes about by reason of the minute hand being placed as it is. In clocks with the minute hand having a separate dial of its own no such unscientific error would have arisen. The second hand in such clocks travels around the dial and points outside the hour numerals.

# CHAPTER VII

# THE BRACKET CLOCK

## CHAPTER VII

### THE BRACKET CLOCK

The term "bracket clock" a misnomer—The great series of English table or mantel clocks—The evolution of styles—Their competition with French elaboration.

LONG-CASE clocks came into being when the long or "royal" pendulum required protection by having a wooden case. It was possible to have a short pendulum, and clocks intended for table use had a short pendulum. The long pendulum swings exactly in a second, and for it to do this it must be of a certain length, determined by physical laws followed according to mechanical formulæ by the scientific clockmaker, too complex to be given here in detail. It may be interesting to record that the length of a seconds pendulum—that is, one requiring one second to move from extreme to extreme—is 39·1398 inches in the latitude of Greenwich and is of different lengths in differing latitudes.

The Term "Bracket Clock" a Misnomer.—In the old form of clock—the brass lantern type, weight-driven—it is obvious that when the weights and chains were suspended below the case the clock could not stand on a table. Such clocks had to hang on a wall, as so many old engravings show, or they were placed on a bracket against a wall, with the weights hanging beneath. With the advent of the pendulum new theories were in the air. At its first use as a short pendulum it was placed in front of the dial. When the seconds pendulum was recognized as a scientific regulator, the length precluded clocks in which it was employed being used as table clocks. It was a distinct departure from miniature timepieces as decorative domestic ornaments. Scientific it undoubtedly was, and as such it commenced a new development in the direction of astronomical clocks and scientific regulators of time. The table clock had to pursue another course. It belongs to another school of mechanism. The weight-driven clock strove to arrive at exactitude and scientific accuracy. The other clock, like the watch, attempted economy of space in conjunction with the maximum of exactitude such economy would allow. It essayed to fulfil certain conditions. It was easily portable, it could stand on a table, or more often on the mantelpiece, a place it can almost claim as its own in the English home by tradition. The watch with similar aims taxed the art of the maker to enable it to be easily carried on the person. These two classes of timepiece, the portable clock and more readily portable watch, were spring-driven. The development of this mechanical principle, running parallel with the evolution of the weight-driven clock,

BRACKET CLOCKS. LATE SEVENTEENTH CENTURY.

Maker, Sam Watson (Coventry). Date, 1687. Maker, Joseph Knibb (Oxon). Date, 1690.
Height, 12 in. Width, 9¾ in. Depth, 6¼ in. Height, 12 in. Width, 8 in. Depth, 5 in.

(*By courtesy of Percy Webster, Esq.*)

BRACKET CLOCKS. EARLY EIGHTEENTH CENTURY.

Maker, Thomas Loomes, at Ye Mermaid in Lothbury. Date, 1700.
Height, 1 ft. 3¾ in. Width, 11¼ in. Depth, 7¼ in.

Maker, Thomas Johnson, Gray's Inn Passage. Date, about 1730.
Height, 1 ft. 2 in. Width, 7 in. Depth, 5 in.

# THE BRACKET CLOCK 185

arrived at great scientific accuracy, as exemplified by the nautical chronometer and by the modern machine-made watch, whose timekeeping qualities are remarkable. In fact, it may be said that the table or portable clock and the watch together have dethroned the weight-driven clock as a domestic clock.

**The Great Series of English Table or Mantel Clocks.—** To the beginner the appearance of an old table clock has not the same enticement as a brass lantern clock with its obvious claim to pre-modern form. It may even be said that the tyro clings reverently to his worship of the "grandfather" clock as something sacred. With their steady, uninterrupted progress from the middle seventeenth century for two hundred years, it is remarkable how conservative these table clocks have been to a comparatively fixed form. They stand in solidarity of workmanship and perfection of mechanical detail as exhibiting the superlative character of English clockmaking. During that period, in long procession, generation after generation, they have upheld the dignity of the science of horology as practised by English clockmakers, whose craftsmanship and perfection of exact detail deservedly won a reputation on the Continent and in America. An English clock of the finest period holds few superiors and very few equals in the world for reliability and exactitude. "*Bajo la palabra de un Inglés*" (On the word of an Englishman) is a proverbial saying in the Spanish States of South America, and such an honourable appellation can

9

equally be applied to the said Englishman's clock, upon which great clockmakers have proudly inscribed their names as guarantee of its fidelity and truth.

From Thomas Tompion in the days of Charles II to Benjamin Vulliamy in the days of George IV the series has been unbroken. We find table clocks by all the leading makers of long-case clocks, so that whatever competition lay between the principles of the one and the principles of the other was confined to the workshop of the clockmaker who set himself to master the intricacies of two styles. It was a friendly rivalry which is found to exist in other fields of human action. Disraeli the politician wrote novels; Macaulay the historian published verse; Seymour Haden laid down his lancet as a doctor to take up the etching-needle to become one of the greatest modern etchers.

**The Evolution of Styles.**—In the examples illustrated, the slow progression of types slightly differing from each other is readily seen. The late seventeenth century exhibits types of reticent form, with ebonized case, and having a brass basket-top decoration surmounted by a handle showing its use as a portable clock. This handle is retained in the carriage clock of to-day—a clock which finds a prototype in the carriage clock of Marie Antoinette. In height these clocks were about 12 inches and in width about 9 inches. At this period brass oblong ornaments were affixed to the case, a detail which disappeared with the next later type.

The clock on the left (illustrated p. 181) is by Sam Watson, of Coventry, and is dated 1687. It has

BRACKET CLOCKS. MID-EIGHTEENTH CENTURY.

Maker, John Page (Ipswich). Date, 1710.
Height, 24 in. Width, 12¾ in. Depth, 5½ in.

Maker, Godfrey Poy (London). Date, 1745.
Height, 26 in. Width, 11 in. Depth, 6¾ in.

(*By courtesy of Percy Webster, Esq.*)

BRACKET CLOCKS. EIGHTEENTH CENTURY (ABOUT 1760).

Maker, Johnson (London).
Height, 1 ft. 5 in. Width, 9¾ in. Depth, 5¼ in.

Maker, Thomas Hill (Fleet Street, London).
Height, 1 ft. 9 in. Width, 1 ft. Depth, 7 in.

## THE BRACKET CLOCK 191

the basket top, reminiscent in decorative treatment of the metal fret found in lantern brass clocks of contemporary date. It will be observed that these clocks have two hands. The spandrels of this and the adjacent clock have the single cherub's-head brass ornament. The latter clock, on the right, is by Joseph Knibb, of Oxford, and is in date 1690. The basket decoration is absent and the top is of simpler form. These two examples indicate that fine work was done in the provinces. By the end of the reign of William III the table clock had grown taller. The example illustrated (p. 183), by Thomas Loomes, is $15\frac{1}{2}$ inches high and $11\frac{1}{2}$ inches wide. It will be noticed that the basket top was still being made, and from now onwards the four turned brass terminals at the top became a feature and lasted for a century. By the first quarter of the eighteenth century a lunette had been added, as shown in the clock on the same page by Thomas Johnson, in date 1730. From this date feet were almost always employed. Similar feet embellished the long clock-case from a slightly later period throughout the century, and are still in evidence in examples made as late as the first half of the nineteenth century. In the 1730 clock by Thomas Johnson, the only brass ornament on the case is the escutcheon to the lock, a feature which, as time went on, lost its prominence and became more reticent.

In the reign of George II the clock again grew in stature. Its portability was evidently not a necessity. It cannot be now said to resemble a carriage clock. Chamber clocks became definite objects of decorative utility as part of the domestic fitments of a room. The architectural ornament becomes pronounced, and there is a massive grandeur about the cases which suited the early Georgian mansions and Hogarthian furniture of the period. These eight-day striking and alarum clocks had become a feature of the English home. The fine provincial example by John Page, of Ipswich, is 24 inches high and $12\frac{1}{4}$ inches wide. In addition to the four terminals there is a fifth at the apex on a column with supporting metal ornament. The adjacent clock by Godfrey Poy, in date 1745, has at the apex a small figure of Ajax. In both these examples there are rings at the side as ornaments, or possibly for use to lift the clock in lieu of the older style of the handle at the top (p. 187).

In the reign of George III (1760–1820) the table clock shows greater variety. It was a restless time, filled with wars and political struggles—a reign notable for the American Declaration of Independence on 4th July 1776, for the beginning of the French Revolution in 1789, for the "darkest hour in English history," the planned invasion of England by French and Spanish fleets, and contemplated invasion of Ireland by the Dutch fleet. In this reign, too, there came what may be termed the industrial revolution due to the introduction of machinery and steam-power. The growing wealth of the middle classes demanded more luxurious furniture. Merchants and manufacturers, shipowners and traders with India and the East, Lancashire cotton-spinners

AMERICAN CLOCK.

With case of fine design in form of lyre, richly gilded and surmounted by eagle.

Makers, Savin & Dyer (Boston). 1780-1800.

(*By courtesy of the Metropolitan Museum of Art, New York.*)

STAFFORDSHIRE COPPER LUSTRE WARE VASE.

With decoration in Chinese style, blue and white, and painted clock dial with no works. Early nineteenth century. The cottager's desire to possess a mantel clock satisfied.

(*In collection of author.*)

## THE BRACKET CLOCK 197

and mill-owners founded a new plutocracy. Bristol and Liverpool traders in "blackbirds," as the iniquitous slave trade was impiously termed, amassed fortunes. Although Pitt advocated the emancipation of slaves, under his rule "the English slave trade more than doubled."

Two George III clocks, in date 1760, by Johnson and by Thomas Hill, are illustrated (p. 189). One shows the recurrence of an old form with the handle at the top of the case, having only as a new feature delicate brackets—a female bust, suggesting in miniature the figure-head of some Indiaman. It is a pleasant ornament one would like to have seen more often adopted. The adjacent clock, by Thomas Hill, evidently derives its design from France, and is a forerunner, in its departure from the square case, of the style which Sheraton, in his adaptation from the French, made at a later date.

**Competition with French Elaboration.**—During the latter decades of the eighteenth and the opening years of the nineteenth centuries, the influx of French fashions had a considerable influence on the furniture designers of this country. What Chippendale had commenced, Sheraton continued, each according to his point of view. So great was the effect that there is actually an English Empire period entirely dependent on the classic interpretation of the French school. To treat of French clocks would occupy a space that is denied in this outline study of English work. But that they are of paramount importance cannot be denied. The French craftsman, as he always did, realized the possibilities of his subject. His cases are elaborate and imaginative in conception. His fertility of invention is remarkable. On the whole it must be admitted that the case is the weakest part of the English clock. The case-maker never quite realized his opportunities. He might have done so much better. There is a stability and solid, almost stolid, soberness that might have been lightened, so one thinks at times. But on the other hand, when the Frenchman is bad in design, his exuberance of ornament and headstrong imagination seem too lurid for a sober clock which only records ordinary time.

This French influence was world-wide. By the courtesy of the authorities of the Metropolitan Museum of Art, New York, an American clock is illustrated (p. 193), the makers being Savin and Dyer, of Boston. This is in date 1780 to 1800. It is of fine proportions, and the lyre ornament is kept in due reticence.

As exemplifying the far-reaching effect that French design had on this country, we reproduce an interesting illustration of a cottager's clock of the early nineteenth cenutry (p. 195). It is really a vase of earthenware made in Staffordshire. On one side is painted in blue a Chinese scene, on the other is a clock-face in imitation of a French dial. But the hands perpetually mark seventeen minutes past eight. In copper lustre-ware this vase with its sham dial served the cottager as something ornamental, although not useful. It is a replica in homely English earthenware of French *finesse*, a cottage echo of the vase-clocks of Sèvres in the

BRACKET CLOCKS. LATE EIGHTEENTH CENTURY.

Maker, Alexander Cumming (London). No maker's name. Date, about 1800.
Date, 1770.
Height, 1 ft. 2 in. Width, 8¼ in. Depth, 5¼ in. Height, 1 ft. 3¾ in. Width, 10½ in. Depth, 6¼ in.

(*By courtesy of Percy Webster, Esq.*)

BRACKET CLOCKS. EARLY NINETEENTH CENTURY. DATE, ABOUT 1805.

Maker, Barraud (London).
Height, 17 in. Width, 12 in. Depth, 6 in.

Maker, Strowbridge (Dawlish).
Height, 16 in. Width, 10 in. Depth, 6½ in.

## THE BRACKET CLOCK 203

apartments at Versailles. The cottager's desire to have a clock was satisfied by the Staffordshire potter.

Many clocks of the last quarter of the eighteenth century show the lingering styles of the earlier decades. It is impossible to lay down any definite rule in furniture, in silver, or in old clocks, that in such a year a certain style ends. Approximately, one may determine periods and by close application discover slight indications of new styles beginning to take the town. Now and again one comes across examples a great many years behind the time, especially in provincial makers, where fashions in cases were not so frequently changed.

Illustrated on p. 199 are two clocks; one, in date 1770, by Alexander Cumming, is only 14 inches in height; the other, 1800, having no maker's name, is 15¾ inches high. A new and very pleasing form is introduced. We see the dial in process of losing its lunette. It makes its ascent on the case to take its place as in later styles. This raising of the dial affected the top of the case, which became of circular form. The transitional period is shown by the ornament remaining in the right-hand clock in the lower spandrels. The case-maker had not quite assimilated the changing form. It is interesting to note that in both these clocks the handles of the early portable clock are reintroduced.

At the beginning of the nineteenth century the circular dial had become established. An interesting transitional clock by Barraud (p. 201), in date 1805, shows that the case-maker was averse to parting with the lunette. He accordingly places the dial in the centre of the case and has a crescent-shaped ornament, with a design adapted by the metal-worker from the Chinese potter. Of the same date is a provincial clock by Strowbridge, of Dawlish. Here the maker has boldly adopted the circular top, and the result is a case of pleasing proportions.

Restlessness of design characterized this period. The old square dial was rarely if ever used. The arched-top case is another form, as illustrated (p. 205), where the maker, Biddell, refrained from following the line of the circular dial in his case. The adjacent example, in date 1800 to 1815, shows the circular dial surmounting the pediment of the case. After its vicissitudes it has at length triumphed in becoming the dominant note in the design.

As illustrating the varied attempts to make the table clock an imposing ornament and deal with its decoration in an elaborate manner, the fine clock in ebony case inlaid with blue and white Wedgwood medallions is a remarkable example (illustrated p. 207). An especially noteworthy feature in this clock is the beaded ornamentation around the dial and the medallions and the other portions of the case of cut steel.

The series of table clocks illustrated should indicate to the reader the salient features of such clocks, which are sought after by collectors and carefully prized by those who love the fine work of the old English clockmakers.

BRACKET CLOCKS.

Maker, Biddell (London). Date, 1800. Enamel dial.
Height, 1 ft. 8 in. Width, 10 in. Depth, 5½ in.

No name of maker. Date, 1810-15.
Height, 1 ft. 7¾ in. Width, 1 ft. Depth, 5¾ in.

EBONY TABLE CLOCK.

Inlaid with medallions of blue and white Wedgwood jasper ware. Enriched with mounted ornament of cut steel.

(*By courtesy of City of Nottingham Museum and Art Gallery.*)

# CHAPTER VIII

# PROVINCIAL CLOCKS

## CHAPTER VIII

### PROVINCIAL CLOCKS

Their character—Names of clockmakers found on clocks in the provinces—The North of England: Newcastle-upon Tyne—Yorkshire clockmakers: Halifax and the district—Liverpool and the district—The Midlands—The Home Counties—The West Country—Miscellaneous makers.

A GREAT deal of attention has been paid by collectors to clocks by well-known London makers and too little examination has been given to fine examples by those of the provinces. In the present chapter an attempt is made to fill a hiatus in this respect, and by the kindness of those interested in the various localities certain data are presented which may stimulate the student to continue his researches on the lines here indicated.

The metropolis attracted noteworthy makers, but they had their origin and often their early training in the provinces.

The following are among the great London clockmakers, but they were not Londoners. They come from all parts of the country. Joseph Knibb (about

1670) was an Oxfordshire man. The famous Thomas Tompion, born in 1638, came from Bedfordshire. George Graham (1673–1751) tramped to London from Cumberland. Thomas Earnshaw, who perfected the marine chronometer, his additions being still in use, was born at Ashton-under-Lyne in 1750 and served his apprenticeship there. Henry Jones, who was the pupil of Edward East, was the son of a vicar at Southampton. Charles II had a clock made by him. Thomas Mudge was the son of a schoolmaster and was born at Exeter in 1715. Another Exeter man was Jacob Lovelace, who took over thirty years to construct a remarkable clock. The celebrated John Harrison was the son of a carpenter on an estate at Pontefract. It was he who competed for the Government gratuity offered for a nautical timekeeper, for which he finally received £10,000, after repeated tests in voyages to the West Indies by himself and his son. We think of his early struggles, when he travelled up to London after he was forty, only to find that he had to return to the provinces and continue his vocation as clock-mender in ordinary and inventor extraordinary. There is a long-case clock with wooden wheels and pinions by him in the Guildhall Museum, London.

The list is by no means complete. There was John Ellicott, who was born at Bodmin, and another Cornishman from the same town is John Arnold, who was apprenticed to his father, a watchmaker there. Arnold continued what Harrison had begun in the chronometer. We must not exclude the great Dr. Hooke, who was born at Freshwater, Isle of

Wight, who invented the anchor escapement for clocks and contested the invention of the balance spring in watches with Huygens.

**Names of Clockmakers found on Clocks in the Provinces.**—It has been suggested that in some cases the name of a local maker does not necessarily determine, when found on the dial or elsewhere, that such clock has been made by the person whose name it bears. It has also been advanced that the name of the owner was sometimes put on the dial. This last theory can be dismissed as being of so infrequent use as to be practically negligible in recording lists of makers. The other conjecture may possibly have sufficient truth in it to disconcert collectors of examples of local crafts. Of course, it is a statement that cannot be proved, nor can it be disproved. Presumably a clockmaker in the eighteenth and early nineteenth centuries, when clockmaking was something more than selling or mending clocks that other people made, did not deliberately set up business and, in a small town where secrecy was impossible, make a practice of putting his name on work he did not execute. That he did not make all the parts himself is admitted. Had he done so, he would have had to be a chain-maker or a catgut-maker, a pulley-maker, a chaser of metal for his dials, a cabinet-maker for his cases, and so on down to his most minute screws. One might as well take similar objection to Sir Joshua Reynolds or Gainsborough that they did not extract their pigments from the natural vegetables or minerals, that they neglected to become proficient in manipulating hogs' bristles or camel-hair into brushes, or that they could not and did not make their own canvases or carve their own frames.

It did happen that an old clock by one maker was sent to another for repair, and he made such extensive repairs to the movement that he felt himself justified in putting his own name to the clock in its new state. The owner would have had something to say to this interchange of names had there not been some justification for it. This practice, however, is not confined to the provinces, and we cannot charge the provincial maker with being wholly unscrupulous.

Some purists in collecting have objected to the presence of a country maker's name stencilled on the dial, as being evidence it was not his handiwork. But this is not in itself a crime. It is far more likely that such a clock is of local make, and that being in a remote part it was not easy to get anyone to paint his name on the dial or engrave it. Had he had it made to order in a town surely his name would have been painted for him. In a measure, crudities of this nature and peculiarities not found in clocks from the great centres are hallmarks of genuineness.

At the time of the passing of the Act in 1797 relating to the taxation of clocks and watches, the following places sent representatives to London to protest against this tax :—

Newcastle-upon-Tyne, Liverpool, Leicester, Derby, Bristol, Prescot, Coventry, and Edinburgh. Of these, Prescot (a few miles from Liverpool) and Coventry represented the watch industry. We may therefore fairly conclude that the other places represent the most noteworthy centres of clockmaking at that period.

**The North of England: Newcastle-upon-Tyne.**—In regard to provincial makers, one wonders what 'prentice hands have gone to the making of the long cases. Did Thomas Chippendale, when he was working at his father's bench at Worcester, execute any of his early joinery and carving to embellish now forgotten clocks? Who can say? At Newcastle-upon-Tyne we are on surer foundation, for it is on record that Thomas Bewick, the wood-engraver, was apprenticed to Ralph Beilby, an engraver at Newcastle, on 1st October 1767 for seven years. His master's business lay in engraving crests and initials on watch seals, teaspoons, sugar-tongs, and other pieces of plate, and the numerals and ornaments on clock dials, together with the maker's name. Here, then, was young Bewick's 'prentice work—the master of white line on the wood block. Later, Bewick confessed to a friend that when engraving these clock dials his hands grew as hard as a blacksmith's, and almost disgusted him with engraving. At any rate, there is the strong probability that such Newcastle dials engraved by Thomas Bewick are on clocks of the date from 1763 to 1774.

The following list of names of Newcastle and other clockmakers in the North of England is produced by the kindness of C. Leo Reid, Esq., of

Newcastle-upon-Tyne, and by the permission of the proprietors of the *Newcastle Weekly Chronicle*, compiled from notes appearing in that valuable repository of North-country antiquities.

The makers are of Newcastle, unless otherwise stated. The list is arranged alphabetically.

John Airey (Hexham), 1790-95.
Jas. Atkinson (Gateshead), 1770-77.
Joseph Atkinson (Gateshead), 1790-1804.
Beilly and Hawthorn, 1780.
William Berry (Gateshead), 1810.
Thomas Bell, 1785.
John Bolton (Chester-le-Street), 1812; (Durham), 1812-21.
S. Boverick, 1765.
William Coventry, 1778.
William Featherstone, 1790-95.
William Fenton, 1778.
William Foggin, 1833 (clock-dial maker).
Gibson, 1750.
John Greaves, 1780-95.
Thomas Greaves, 1778-95.
John Harrison, 1790-95.
John Hawthorn, 1780.
W. Heron, 1790.
Geo. Hidspeth, 1800.
J. Hutchinson, 1811.
Matt. Kirkup, 1811.
Jos. Ledgard, 1707-32.
Richard Marshall (Wolsingham), 1796.
Geo. Miller (Gateshead), 1770.
Sam Ogden, 1760-70.

Ord (Hexham), 1797.
Jno. Peacock, 1800.
John Rawson, 1790.
Wm. Rawson, 1790.
Christian Ker Reid, 1778-1834. St. Nicholas Churchyard, close to workshop of Thomas Bewick.
Reid and Son, 1817.
Reid and Sons, 1845 to present day.
Henry Sanders (Gateshead), 1800.
John Scott (Sandgate), 1790-95.
Thomas Smoult, 1790.
Hugh Stockell, 1790.
Stockell and Stuart, 1798.
Hugh Stockell, 1800.
Archibald Strachan, 1790.
William Tickle, sen., 1790-95.
William Tickle, jun., 1790-95.
J. H. Wakefield (Gateshead), 1800.
John Wakefield (Lamesley), 1827.
Ward, 1811.
Michael Watson, 1811-27.
Thomas Weatherley (Berwick-on-Tweed), 1790-95.
John Weatherston, 1790-95.
John Wilson, 1782-90.
Richard Young, 1811.

In regard to the remarks about Thomas Bewick and clock dials, there is every likelihood that his 'prentice work in engraving them between 1763 and 1774 is to be found on clocks by S. Boverick, William Coventry, William Fenton, Gibson, John Hawthorn, John Wilson, and Christian K. Reid; the latter maker certainly knew Bewick. The dates given in the above list do not definitely represent that the maker's work was confined to that period exclusively. They are approximate dates.

**Yorkshire Clockmakers: Halifax and the District.**—We have already seen that John Harrison, the great self-taught genius, born in 1683, was a Yorkshireman. Of early makers there is a record of John Ogden, of Bowrigg, of the late seventeenth century, and Samuel Ogden, born at Sowerby in 1669. The name of Ogden is found on many Yorkshire clocks. Thomas Ogden came to Halifax; although the Ogdens seem to have been a Quaker family, one of his clocks is in the Unitarian Chapel vestry. The Ogden type of dial with the phases of the moon, although not original, being adapted from Dutch models, became noteworthy in the North of England, and such styles were termed "Halifax" clocks. Samuel Ogden, a descendant, migrated to Newcastle-upon-Tyne (see list, p. 216), perpetuating the name a hundred years after.

In Halifax parish churchyard is a tombstone to the memory of R. Duckworth, clockmaker, 1677.

John Mason was a maker about 1760, and his father, Timothy Mason, was a clockmaker before him. At Rotherham some years ago there were some Mason clocks on exhibition, and there were eight generations of Masons as clockmakers, the later branch having settled at Rotherham. Such is the record of many provincial makers.

Emanuel Hopperton, of Leeds, made clocks with marquetry cases. One bore the proud motto, *Non mihi sed mundo.*

Henry Brownhill, of Briggate, Leeds, watchmaker and clockmaker, was sufficiently prosperous to issue several tons of halfpenny copper tokens in 1793. By the courtesy of S. H. Hamer, Esq., of Halifax, an illustration of one of these tokens is given.

This was the year when the Reign of Terror

HALFPENNY, 1793.

began and when Marie Antoinette was executed. In England great commercial distress was felt. Banks issued notes in excess of their capital. Gold was scarce, and the Bank of England restricted its issues. A panic ensued and several banks failed. Pitt issued Exchequer Bills to the extent of five millions.

Other local clockmakers are Thomas Liston, of Luddenden, 1718–79, and his son Thomas, of Halifax, 1745–1815. It is reported that this latter Thomas Lister travelled by coach from Halifax to

LONG-CASE CLOCK. ENLARGEMENT OF HOOD.
Maker, Gilbert Chippindale (Halifax). Showing fine fretwork and maker's name in lunette.

(*By courtesy of Surgeon-Major W. Savile Henderson.*)

LONG-CASE EIGHT-DAY CLOCK.

Maker, John Weatherilt (Liverpool).
Date, 1780–85.

(*Reproduced by courtesy of George H. Hewitt, Esq., J.P.*)

London to regulate and keep in order the clock at St. Paul's Cathedral. There is an orrery by him in the Glasgow University Museum.

William Lister is another member of the same family who made long-case clocks. In his dials a noticeable feature is the absence of the hour circle as being separate from the rest of the plate. The dial was made in one piece and attached to a back-plate of brass.

Pattison, another Yorkshire maker, made long-case clocks similar to those of William Lister.

John Hartley, of Halifax, about 1770, was the maker of a thirty-hour grandfather clock in oak case with brass square dial and moon and date lunettes. Titus Bancroft, of Sowerby Bridge, 1822, a church-clock maker, also made grandfather clocks.

John Hallifax, of Barnsley, who died in 1750, made a fine long-case clock now at Wentworth House.

Gilbert Chippindale, of Halifax, 1781, is another maker of fine clocks. A fine example of his work is illustrated (p. 219).

R. Henderson, of Scarborough, early eighteenth century, is another Yorkshire maker. Richard Midgley, 1720–40, of Halifax, made a number of clocks still treasured locally. Samuel Pearson is known about 1790, and John Stancliffe, of Bark-island, is another local maker.

Collectors have too frequently associated Yorkshire clocks with the later periods, with ponderous cases of gigantic size, but, as is shown, the Yorkshire makers are worthy of considerable attention by connoisseurs as having a lineage extending back into the periods when clockmaking was at its best, and when the case-maker was not such a preponderating factor as he seems to have been in the early nineteenth-century days in the North.

**Liverpool and the District.**—In regard to Liverpool and the vicinity, at the Ter-centenary Historical Exhibition at the Walker Art Gallery in 1907 a collection of clocks and watches was made to illustrate the art of the clockmaker in that part of the country. By the kindness of George H. Hewitt, Esq., J.P., who arranged these exhibits, we are enabled to supply the names of many of the Liverpool clockmakers.

Peter Litherland patented the rack lever escapement in 1793-4 which Robert Roskell, the Liverpool maker, introduced into his watches. At the above Exhibition was shown a pendulum watch by George Taylor, about 1700, and one by William Tarleton, 1797, with the Government stamp indicating that the tax of a guinea had been paid. This was in 1797, the first and only year when a tax on watches and clocks was levied. One remembers the fine portrait of Colonel Tarleton in uniform, with one foot on a cannon, after the portrait by Sir Joshua Reynolds, signed I. Johnson, on a Liverpool mug. He was the Member of Parliament for Liverpool from 1790 to 1812. This family gave the name to Tarleton Street, Liverpool.

That Liverpool and the district was renowned for its watches is shown by a silver watch made by Thomas Worsley, Liverpool, inscribed, " Presented to Robert Burns by his brother ploughmen of Air

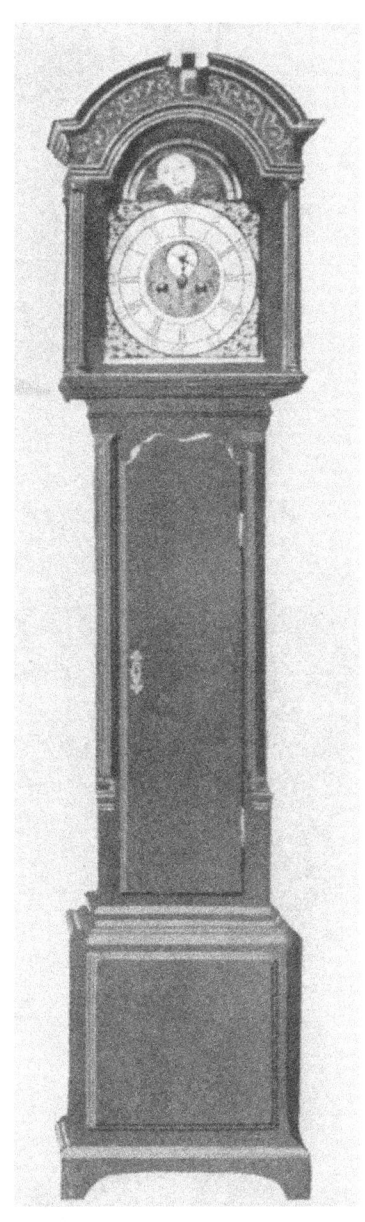

LONG-CASE EIGHT-DAY CLOCK.

Maker, Thurston Lassell (Toxteth Park, Liverpool).
Date, about 1745.

(*Reproduced by courtesy of George H. Hewitt, Esq., J.P.*)

LONG-CASE MAHOGANY EIGHT-DAY CLOCK.

Maker, Henry Higginbotham (Macclesfield).
The Gothic panel in door is a noticeable feature.

(*By courtesy of A. Bromley Sanders, Esq., Exeter.*)

(*sic*) March 9, 1785." Among other makers at Liverpool whose names are found on watches are Fairclough (about 1800), Edmonds (about 1770), Joseph Finney (about 1770), Robert Roskell (about 1800), M. J. Tobias & Co. (1820), Harrington (1790), Peter Hope (1795), J. Johnson (1796).

It is possible that some of these makers also made long-case and other clocks; we find the name of Roskell on a long-case clock and R. Roskell on another. Presumably this was the Robert Roskell who used the Litherland rack-lever watch escapement. Joseph Finney also made long-case clocks. Other makers' names found on Liverpool clocks are Burges, Aspinall (with the motto, " Time is valuable "), Jno. Weatherilt. This clock is illustrated (p. 221). It indicates by the character of its marquetry in the panel of the door and in the base that it belongs to the second period of marquetry contemporary with the influence of Sheraton. In the lunette the phases of the moon are shown. The date of this is about 1780 to 1785. Another clock, illustrated on p. 225, is by Thurston Lassell, Toxteth Park, Liverpool. This in date is about 1745. The phases of the moon are shown in the lunette. The case is of more slender proportions than its fellow. The hood exhibits a reticence which was lost in later examples, especially in provincial work made in Yorkshire, where the case became of unwieldy size and somewhat ungainly shape.

Other names of Liverpool makers found on long-case clocks are William Sutton, Harrison & Son, Jas. Canson, Thomas Saxon, Jo[n] Taylor (Ormskirk),

W. Lassell, Toxteth Park, Liverpool, with motto, "Time shows the Way of Life's Decay," with brass face, lunar movement, and monthly dial with indicator. (This style of dial is a feature of a Shropshire clock illustrated p. 249.) Brown, Liverpool, is found on a mahogany long-case clock and also on a small long-case clock. To those who are interested the portrait in oils of Peter Litherland, the inventor of the rack lever, who died in 1804, is in the possession of the Corporation of Liverpool.

Among other Lancashire makers the following are noteworthy: T. Lees (Bury), 1795–1800; Archibald Coats (Wigan), 1780; Barr (Bolton), 1790; James Barlow (Oldham), 1775; Benjamin Barlow (Ashton-under-Lyne), 1780; and Nathaniel Brown (Manchester), 1780–1785.

In Westmorland and Cumberland the names Burton, of Kendal, and Russell, of Carlisle, are often found on grandfather clocks of local manufacture of the late eighteenth century.

In regard to a particular style of case associated with Lancashire and with Cheshire, having the door decorated with panel in Gothic style, two examples are illustrated (p. 227), one by Henry Higginbotham (Macclesfield), and the other by Heywood, Northwich, 1790 (p. 231).

**Clockmakers of the Midlands.**—As typical of the fine work produced, the bracket clock by Sam Watson, of Coventry, 1687, illustrated (p. 181), shows that the provincial maker was at that date in no way on a lower plane than his contemporary in London. Other makers are Wilson (Warwick), 1709; John

LONG-CASE MAHOGANY EIGHT-DAY CLOCK.

Maker, Heywood (Northwich, Cheshire). 1790.
The Gothic panel in door is a noticeable feature.

(*By courtesy of Messrs. A. B. Daniell & Sons.*)

LONG-CASE EIGHT-DAY CLOCK.

With dial showing days of month. Oak case veneered in mahogany.

Maker, Thomas Wall (Birmingham). Date, about 1795.

(*In possession of author.*)

Whitehurst (Derby), 1785—a fine long-case clock by this maker is in the Metropolitan Museum of Art, New York; W. Francis (Birmingham), and Thomas Wall (Birmingham), 1798. An example by this maker is illustrated (p. 233), exhibiting a pastoral scene painted in the lunette of the dial. This clock—in the possession of the author—keeps excellent time although 120 years old, and has gone for ten years without stopping.

Of Nottingham makers, the following names of early craftsmen are found on watches: Isaac Alexander, about 1760 (a watch, gold inner case, white dial; outer case of shagreen, with portrait of Charles Stuart by J. June, 1745), and Thomas Hudson, about 1790 (silver, white dial; outer case of tortoiseshell, with silver mounts). The name of Hen. Page, Upper Broughton (Notts), is found on a brass clock, and John Kirk was a maker at Epperstone and Skegby before he came to London in 1677 and was admitted as a member of the Clockmakers' Company. Among the collection of watches at Nottingham Museum, apart from the two above-mentioned, are a good many by makers of a later date, mainly of the early nineteenth century: John Lingford, A. Shepperley, William Young—all of Nottingham, and Geo. Stacey, Worksop.

Among the other watches on exhibition are an early one by Robert Dent (Lincoln), No. 61, and a watch with gold case with chased *repoussé* figures and ornament by J. Windmills, the celebrated London maker, 1671–1700.

This short list of Midland makers is obviously

incomplete, and it is to be hoped that some painstaking horologists will amplify it and do honour to the makers and to the counties concerned.

**The Home Counties.**—Thomas Tompion (1671–1713), the famous London maker, commenced at Bedford and ended at Bath. We have seen a brass lantern clock engraved "Thos. Tonkink de Bedforde." This might very well be one of his early clocks, and we know his great last triumph in the famous long-case clock in the Pump Room at Bath. But apart from this incidental connection of the "father of English watchmaking" with the provinces, there stands Joseph Knibb, of Oxon, who was admitted

to the Clockmakers' Company of London in 1677. He worked in London for the Court of Charles II. But he was established in Oxfordshire, as is shown by the copper token he issued, with inscription "Joseph Knibb Clockmaker in Oxon," and on reverse the dial of a clock with initials I.K. in centre. We give an illustration of this token.

A long-case eight-day clock finely decorated in marquetry, in date about 1690, is illustrated (p. 237). This exhibits the work of Knibb as being equal, as his employment at the Court shows, to the leading London makers of his day. In the chapter on Marquetry, p. 79, will be found a notice of this

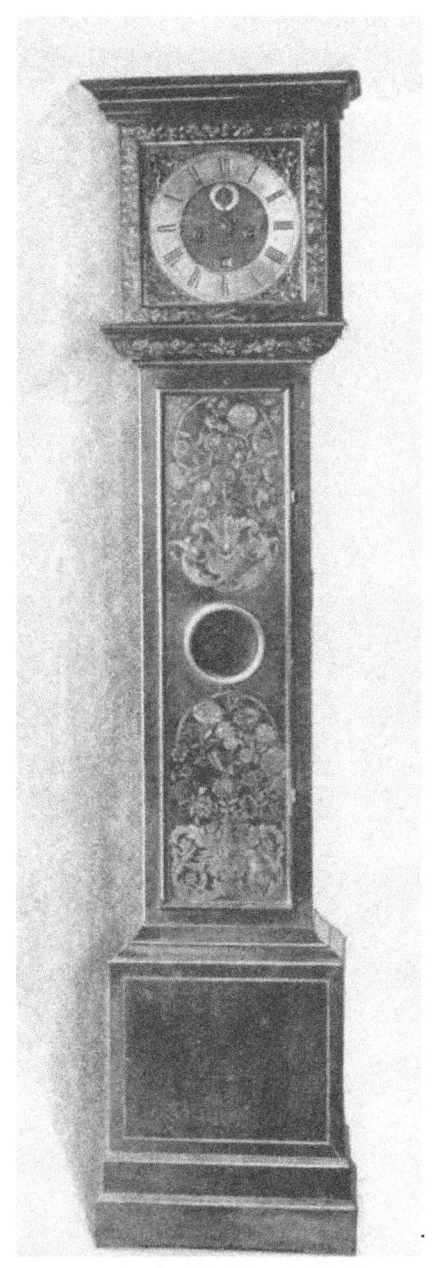

LONG-CASE EIGHT-DAY CLOCK.

Decorated in marquetry.
Maker, Joseph Knibb (Oxon). Date about 1690.

GEORGIAN SPANISH MAHOGANY LONG-CASE CLOCK.

Hood enriched with fretwork in Chinese style of Chippendale.
Terminals of carved mahogany.

Maker, Cockey (Warminster).

*(By courtesy of Messrs. D. Sherratt & Co., Chester.)*

# PROVINCIAL CLOCKS 241

clock in regard to its relation to other styles of marquetry, and its place in the sequence there described.

A fine bracket clock by Joseph Knibb, in date about 1690, is illustrated (p. 181). This is of the same period as the long-case clock, the year when William of Orange defeated James II at the battle of the Boyne, and James, the last of the Stuarts, fled into France. It is possible that the fortunes of Joseph Knibb were bound up with Whitehall. At the Revolution in 1689 our Court clockmaker no doubt retreated into Oxfordshire to continue his creations which we now know. A cloud of unpaid debts must have hung over him, for the Stuarts were bad paymasters.

**The West Country.**—In publishing lists of clockmakers collected by local antiquaries, a loyal service has been rendered to the West Country by the *Devon and Cornwall Notes and Queries*. The following list is based on the researches published in that journal by R. Pearse-Chope, Esq.,[1] and by H. Tapley-Soper, Esq.[2]

Balle, John (Exeter).
Bickle, R. H. (Bishop's Nympton).
Bradford (Tiverton).
Bradford (Drayford).
Braund, John (Hatherleigh).
Brayley and Street (Bridgwater).
Bucknell, Jas. (Crediton).
Chamberlain, Hen. (Tiverton).
Chasty, Robert (Hatherleigh).
Chasty, William (Teignmouth).
Day, Christopher (South Molton).

Drake, R. (Beaminster).
Eastcott, Richard (Exon).
Edward, Clement, *c.* 1671.
Ezekiel (Exon), *c.* 1794.
Follet (Sidmouth).
Foster, James (Ashburton).
Fox, John (Alverton).
Gard, Henry (Exeter).
Gard, William (Exeter).
Gaydon, J. (Barnstaple).
Gould (Bishop's Nympton).

---

[1] 1912-13, p. 242.  [2] 1914-15, pp. 204, 205; and July 1917.

Gould, G. (South Molton).
Harding, Charles (Sidmouth).
Harner (Membury).
Hayward, Peter (Crediton), c. 1766.
Howard, Wm., 1760.
Hutchins, William (Cullompton).
Huxtable (Chittlehampton).
Huxtable, E. (South Molton).
Jacobs, A. (Torquay).
Jonas, Saml. (Exon), 1783.
Keffutt, Walter (Exon).
Lord, John (Farringdon).
Lovelace, Jacob (Exeter), died 1766.
Mallett, Peter, 1705.
Mallett, John (Barnstaple), 1840.
March, R. (Honiton).
Otercey, John (Torrington).
Passmore, R. (Barnstaple).
Pile, Fra. (Honiton).
Pollard (Crediton), 1760.
Pollard, Thomas (Exeter).
Price (Wiveliscombe).
Rew, Joseph (Wiveliscombe).
Routledge, George (Lydford), died 1801.
(Epitaph Lydford Churchyard.)
Sanderson, Geo. (Exeter).
(Maker and patentee of tools for duplicating parts of watches, 1761.)
Scoble, John S. (Colyton).
Simons, A. (Bideford).
Skinner (Exon).
Snell, E. (Barnstaple).
Stocker (Honiton).
Strowbridge (Dawlish).
Stumbel (Totnes).
Thorn (South Molton).
Thorne, Sim (Tiverton), 1740.
Thorne, Michl. (South Molton).
Tickle, John (Crediton), 1730.
Upjohn, Richard (Exon).
(Long-case clock, c. 1730.)
Upjohn, Wm. (Exeter), 1741.
Upjohn, Peter (Bideford).
(Watch, 1780.)
Weller, Geo. (Exon).
Wood, I. (Exon).
Waldron, John (Tiverton).

Dates from church registers, family Bibles, old wills, marriage records, and old newspapers to amplify local lists such as this add greatly to their value in establishing period of clock.

Jacob Lovelace, of Exeter, who died in 1766, was the maker of a remarkable clock of most elaborate nature, with organ that played, and a series of moving figures striking the hours, and bellringers and other intricate diversions. This clock was exhibited at the International Exhibition in 1851, and is now at the Liverpool Museum.

A fine long-case clock in Chippendale style by Cockey, of Warminster, is illustrated (p. 239), and exhibits provincial work both in case and movement of the highest character.

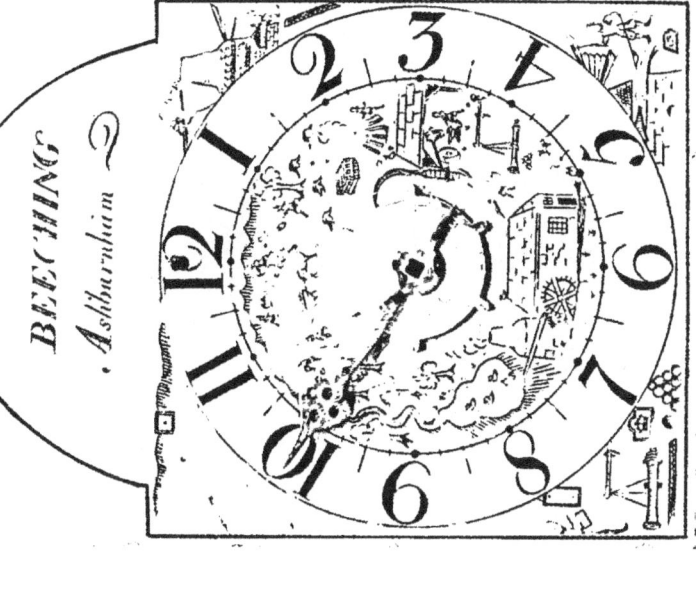

IRON DIAL OF THIRTY-HOUR CLOCK.

Single hand and alarum. Mid-eighteenth century. Ornamented with designs of various phases of Sussex iron industry. Maker, Beeching (Ashburnham).

(*From the collection of J. C. Dawson, Esq., F.S.A.*)

BRASS DIAL OF CLOCK.

By Shenkyn Shon (Blackcock Inn, Pontnedd Fechan). 1714.

(*At National Museum of Wales, Cardiff.*)

LONG-CASE CLOCK WITH RARE OVAL DIAL.

Subsidiary seconds and calendar dials. Blue painted decoration, under glass, in spandrels above dial. Fine carved work in oval frame.

Maker, Marston (Salop). Brass plate on door dated 1761.

*(By courtesy of Walter Idris, Esq.)*

Strowbridge, of Dawlish, is the maker of a bracket clock, in date about 1805, showing pleasing work in the fine marquetry decoration introduced by Sheraton (illustrated p. 201). There is an instance on record of a clock being sent to " Mr. Strowbridge " for repair. "When it came back his name, ' H. Strowbridge, Dawlish,' was engraved upon the dial."

**Miscellaneous Makers — East Anglia.** — Several makers are connected with Yarmouth. There is Thomas Utting (Yarmouth), and we have seen a fine long-case clock signed thus, and there is Isaac Johnson (Yarmouth), who apparently made wall clocks. John Page, of Ipswich, is the maker of a very handsome bracket clock, in date about 1740 (illustrated p. 187). The name of Henry Terold, Ipswich, is found on a round silver watch with chased interlacing bands and silver dial, of seventeenth-century period. Joseph Chamberlain, of Norwich, is a name found on a late seventeenth-century watch. The names of Mann and Jon. Nevill, both of Norwich, are found on late eighteenth-century grandfather clocks.

**Kent and Sussex.** — The name of William Gill or Gilt, of Maidstone, is found on a fine long-case clock of the eighteenth century. William Gardner, of Sandwich, and Joseph Carswell, of Hastings, are other names found on grandfather clocks of the latter part of the eighteenth century. The dial of a clock by a Sussex maker, Beeching, of Ashburnham, from a thirty-hour clock with single hand and alarum (illustrated p. 243), is of mid-eighteenth century period, and shows in its decorations the various phases of the iron industry carried on at Ashburnham.

Welsh Clocks.—At the Amgueddfa Genedlaethol Cymru, at Cardiff, the National Museum of the Principality, there is a long-case clock by B. C. Vaughan, of Pontypool, and a brass block with movement by "Shenkyn Shon, Black Cock Inn, Pontnedd Fechan, 1714," and also there exhibited are the works of the old clock from St. David's Cathedral.

Illustrated on p. 245 is a unique long-case clock with brass plate on door, with date 1761, with dragon above. The particular feature of especial interest in this clock is its oval dial (which is separately illustrated, p. 249). This dial is enamelled white, and has a medallion at top representing the figure of Hope with an anchor. The other decoration is interesting as exhibiting the attempt of the provincial maker to simulate in pigment the marquetry work of the Sheraton school, the design being similar to that found on tea-caddies, no doubt well known to the painter of the dial. There are two subsidiary dials, one for seconds and the other showing the days of the month.

Although the maker's name is "Marston (Salop)" there is an especially Welsh interest attaching to this clock. It once was in the possession of Daniel Owen, the famous Welsh novelist, who is buried in Mold churchyard, and whose monument is in the County Hall Field at Mold. He introduced this clock into his novel, *Rhys Lewis*. The grandmother of the youthful hero of the story had gone to the fair; in her absence the boy took this clock to pieces, so the story goes. But as the hours wore on he found it was easier to take it to pieces

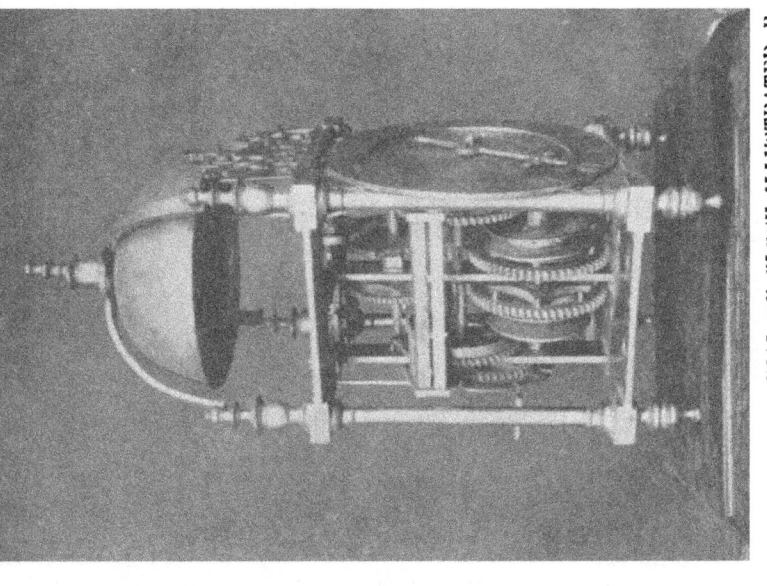

DIAL OF CLOCK ILLUSTRATED P. 233.

Lunette painted with figure subject of woman and pitcher at stream. Spandrels decorated with roses in red and gold.

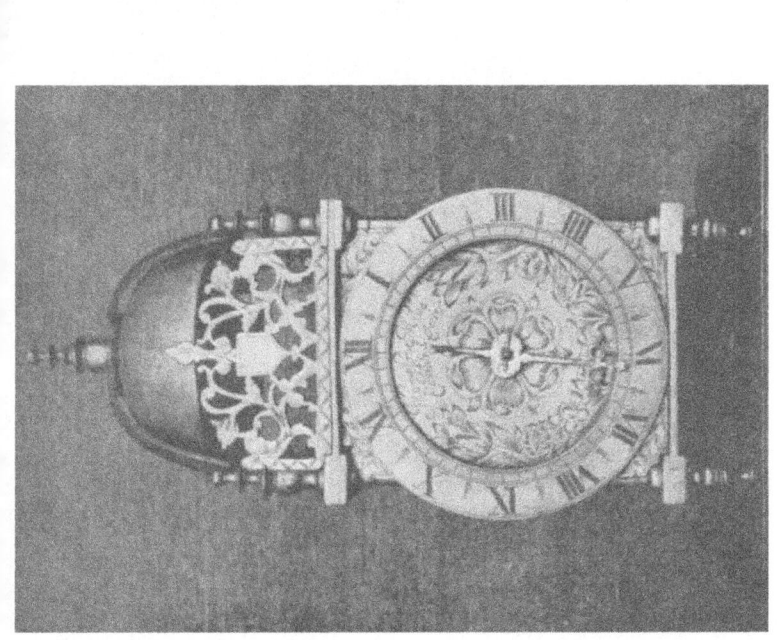

DIAL OF CLOCK ILLUSTRATED P. 245.

This oval form is rare. The Sheraton type of decoration painted on dial is a noticeable feature. The panel is reminiscent of Pergolesi. The lower dial indicates the days of month.

than to put it together again.  The scene on the return of his grandmother is piquantly described. The clockwork ran like a thing demented, and the tell-tale hands revealed the secret of the culprit, who uneasily fingered a missing wheel in his pocket, and he had forgotten to put on the pendulum.

The hood of the clock is of original decoration. The upper spandrels have a blue-and-gold floral design, covered with glass.  The two lower spandrels are delicately carved.  The frame around the oval dial is of beaded work cut in broad and effective style.

Altogether this clock possesses features appealing to collectors.  The provincial maker followed his own lines, and has in so doing produced something unique.

In conclusion, some apology should be made for an attempt to sketch in makers of repute, scattered over so wide an area, which resulted in a mere outline. The meagre lists may in many cases be said to be noteworthy for their omissions.  But want of space has precluded the writer from pursuing the subject further, and he may be permitted to express a hope that the perusal of these facts may stimulate local efforts to worthier records.

# CHAPTER IX

# SCOTTISH AND IRISH CLOCKS

## CHAPTER IX

### SCOTTISH AND IRISH CLOCKS

David Ramsay, Clockmaker Extraordinary to James I—Some early "knokmakers"—List of eighteenth-century Scottish makers—Character of Scottish clocks—Irish clockmakers: Dublin, Belfast, Cork—List of Irish clockmakers.

AMONG the most notable of the early Scottish makers was David Ramsay, who was clockmaker to James VI of Scotland and followed that monarch to London. In Sir Walter Scott's *Fortunes of Nigel*, Ramsay is introduced as a character. "David Ramsay by name, who, whether recommended by his great skill in his profession, as the courtiers alleged, or, as was murmured among his neighbours, by his birthplace, in the good town of Dalkeith, near Edinburgh, held in James's household the post of maker of watches and horologes to his Majesty. He scorned not, however, to keep open shop within Temple Bar, a few yards to the eastward of St. Dunstan's Church."

It appears that he was of a mystical turn of mind, and conceived the idea of treasure buried in the cloisters of Westminster Abbey. Dean Withnam gave permission to dig, and prudently stipulated as a condition that he came in for a share. One John Scott, pretending to the skilled use of the divining rod, Ramsay, and several others, according to the astrologer Lilly in his *Life and Times*, dug 6 feet deep with the aid of labourers and came to a coffin, but as it was not heavy they did not open it, " which we afterwards much repented." When at this impious task a terrific storm arose, and " we verily believed the west end of the church would have fallen upon us." Candles and torches, except one, were extinguished. " John Scott, my partner, was amazed, looked pale, knew not what to think or do until I gave directions and command to dismiss the demons ; which when done, all was quiet again, and each man returned unto his lodging late, about twelve o'clock at night." The share of the Dean in the treasure therefore came to nought.

The *Dictionary of National Biography* supplements and corrects Sir Walter. " Clockmaker Extraordinary " was Ramsay's title, and his son says: " When James I succeeded to the crown of England, he sent into France for my father, who was there, and made him page of the bedchamber and keeper of his Majesty's clocks and watches."

He was of considerable reputation, as, when the charter of incorporation was granted by Charles I to the Clockmakers' Company of London, he was appointed as the first master in 1631. He apparently was not of a worldly disposition, and it is believed

## SCOTTISH AND IRISH CLOCKS 257

that when the destinies of the Stuarts were under a cloud he was in great poverty. His son writes of his father: " It's true your carelessness in laying up while the sun shone for the tempests of a stormy day, hath given occasion to some inferior spirited people not to value you for what you are by nature and in yourself, for such look not to a man longer than he is in prosperity, esteeming none but for their wealth, not wisdom, power, nor virtue."

The knowledge of what manner of man was this old Scottish clockmaker adds a pleasure to the contemplation of his work. At the Guelph Exhibition were shown a clock and alarum watch with single hand, dated 1636, signed *D. Ramsay*. This was on the eve of the Civil War, a year before Hampden refused to pay ship money in England and the introduction of a new Prayer Book in Scotland. But the Prayer Book was no sooner opened at St. Giles's, Edinburgh, than a murmur ran through the congregation, and the murmur soon grew into a formidable riot. The Covenant signed in the churchyard of the Greyfriars at Edinburgh set a flame alight throughout Scotland. "Such was the zeal of subscribers that for a while many subscribed with tears on their cheeks "—some were indeed reputed to have " drawn their own blood and used it in place of ink to underwrite their names."

In such times old David Ramsay, away in the South, saw Stuart magnificence come to a close. At the British Museum is a watch he signs " *David Ramsay, Scotus me fecit.*" In signing thus, he shows he was proud of being a Scotsman, and as a great

Scottish clockmaker his name and record are given the place of honour at the front of this sketch of Scottish work. His watches are richly decorated in the French style; doubtless he learned his craft in France. His last years were passed in the stormy period of the Revolution, and he lived to see Cromwell and the Roundheads defeat Leslie at Dunbar. He died in Holborn in 1654, the year of the union of England and Scotland under Cromwell by Ordinance.

**Some Early "Knokmakers."**—A clock in Scottish is a *knok*. It would appear that the early "knokmakers" were more conversant with the Kirk knok, the Tolbooth knok, and the College knok, than with the domestic clock or watch.

In the middle of the seventeenth century, as in England at a slightly previous date, clockmakers formed themselves into trade guilds. London was incorporated in 1631. Edinburgh followed in 1646, Glasgow, 1649, Haddington, 1753, and Aberdeen not till 1800. The metal-workers of Scotland have always been renowned, and at the above dates clockmakers were eligible to enter the Hammermen's Incorporations as affiliated with the craft of locksmith, which was of ancient lineage.

During the seventeenth century the Scottish clockmakers, in common with English, came under foreign inspiration. But the eighteenth century saw a complete school of makers springing up in various parts of the country, flowing to, and again flowing from, Edinburgh and the Canongate (including Leith), which were the earliest centres of Scottish clockmaking.

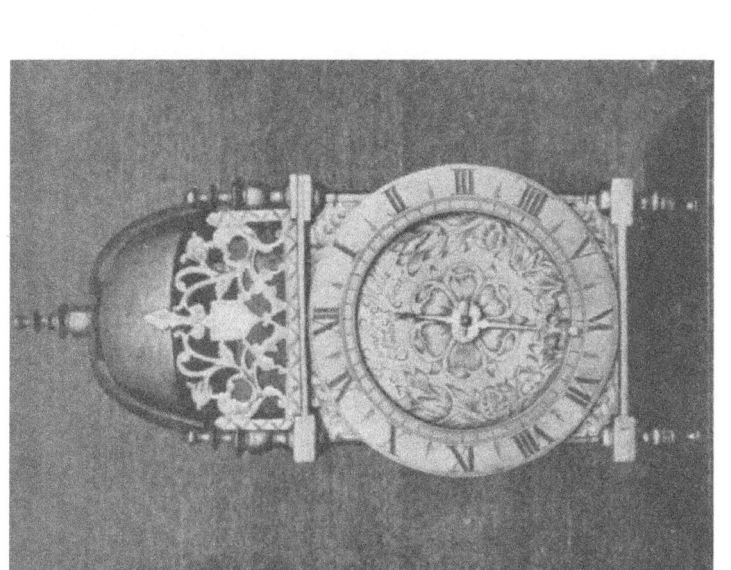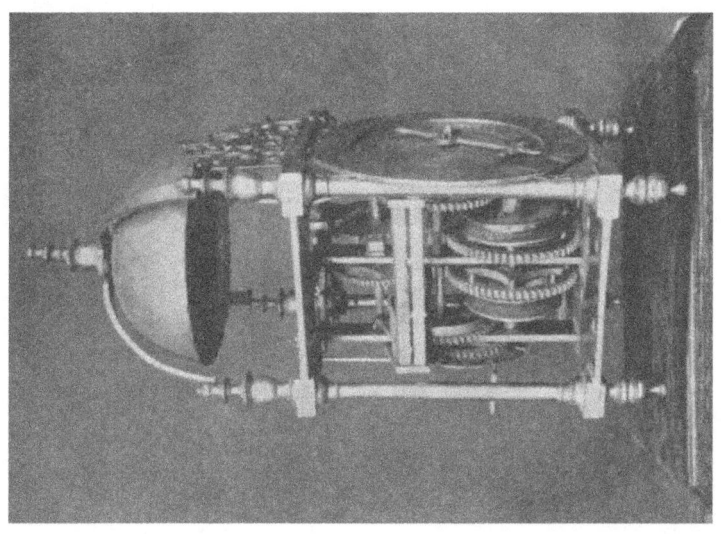

BRASS LANTERN CLOCK.

With brass dial and fine fretwork. Inscribed "Humphry Mills at Edinburgh Fecit." Date, about 1670.
(*In the Glasgow Museum. Reproduced by permission of the Glasgow Corporation.*)

## SCOTTISH AND IRISH CLOCKS 261

We mention a few of the early makers. There was Humphry Mills, who is referred to in the minutes of the Incorporation of Hammermen, Edinburgh, in 1661. There is an example of his work in the Antiquarian Museum, Edinburgh, and we illustrate another in the Corporation Museum at Glasgow (p. 259). This lantern clock, with brass dial and fine fretwork with floriated design, is inscribed *Humphry Mills at Edinburgh fecit*.

Richard Mills, or Milne, was apparently the nephew of Humphry, and was admitted a freeman clockmaker at Edinburgh in 1678. He died in 1710. Another early maker is John Alexander, of Edinburgh, made a freeman in 1671, his trial being to make "ane Knok and mounting and ane sun dyall," also a "Kist lock and key," this part of the locksmith's craft being one of the necessary proofs of craftsmanship for admission as a fully qualified Hammerman. He died in 1707. It is interesting to note that he had to construct a sundial. The art of dialling is intricate, and this indicates that the old clockmaker had a sound technical and scientific knowledge. He was evidently no maker of clocks as "bits o' mechanism," or an assembler of parts. He understood principles.

Thomas Gordon, apprentice to Andrew Brown, Edinburgh, 1688, was in business for forty years and died in 1743. His nephew, Patrick Gordon, was the son of Alexander Gordon, of Briggs, and seems to have been a man of wealth, apart from his trade as a clockmaker. A fine example of his work is illustrated (p. 263), a long-case clock having the door of lacquered work in the "Chinese taste." On the case without the panel is stencilled work, attempting to follow out the style of the imported panel. This example indicates what has already been advanced in the chapter on Lacquered Cases (pp. 110, 114), that such work was of foreign origin. This panelled door is of oak.

Other seventeenth-century makers include Paul Roumieu, 1677 to 1694, the first practical watchmaker who came to Edinburgh. Before that date only clocks were attempted.

Paul Roumieu, jun., son of the above, was admitted as a freeman of Edinburgh in 1692, and died in 1710.

**List of Eighteenth-century Scottish Makers.**—In regard to the activities of Scottish clockmakers in comparison with their fellow-craftsmen across the border, it is interesting to note that there are very few examples of the early crown and verge escapement by Scotch makers, but there are a great number of the anchor escapement. Although invented by Hooke in 1675, this was not taken up readily. This unwillingness to adopt new styles is a feature in clockmaking in the provinces and in Scotland. The works of a clock are not unfrequently put by the maker into a case belonging to a period of cabinet work of some forty years previous. The clockmaker was an autocrat, and compelled the case-maker to follow old traditions in making cases.

The following names of noted makers of the eighteenth century are usually found on long-case clocks of the grandfather type:—

LONG-CASE CLOCK.

With door decorated in lacquer; remainder of case finished in stencil.

Maker, Patrick Gordon, Edinburgh (1705-15).

(*By courtesy of Edward Campbell, Esq., Glasgow.*)

# SCOTTISH AND IRISH CLOCKS 265

Richard Alcorn (Edinburgh), 1703-39 (died).
Thomas Ancrum (Edinburgh).
Apprenticed 1703 to Andrew Brown.
Andrew Brown (Edinburgh), 1665-1711 (died).
Apprenticed to Humphry Milne.
Alexander Brownlie (Edinburgh), 1710-39 (died).
Hugh Campbell (Edinburgh).
Apprenticed to Humphry Milne 1692.
James Cowan (Edinburgh), 1744-81 (died).
John Dalgleish (Edinburgh), 1742-70 (died).
Alexander Ferguson (Dundee), 1777.
Jos. Gibson (Ecclefechan), about 1750 (see illustration, p. 267).
Patrick Gordon (Edinburgh), 1699-1749 (died).
Thomas Gordon (Edinburgh), 1688-1743 (died).
James Greig (Perth), 1773-76.
Thomas Hogg (Edinburgh).
Apprenticed to Andrew Brown 1698.

{ Anthony Hopton (Edinburgh).
Matthew Hopton (Edinburgh).
Makers of wooden clocks 1799-1817.
John Hopton.
Carried on business to 1850. }
John Kerr (Glasgow), 1783.
Andrew Lyon (Port Glasgow), 1783.
Geo. Munro (Canongate), 1750-99.
Thomas Reid (Edinburgh), 1762-1831 (died).
Author of *Treatise on Clock and Watchmaking*, 1826.
John Russell (Falkirk), 1797-1818 (died).
Geo. Skelton (Edinburgh), 1773-1834 (died).
John Smith (Pittenweem, Fife).
Self-taught. Came to Edinburgh in 1774. Maker of musical clocks, etc. Disposed of his clocks by lottery in 1809 at Edinburgh.
Archibald Straiton (Edinburgh), 1739-84 (died).
Wm. Sutor (Edinburgh), 1712-15.
William Veitch (Haddington), 1758.
James Young (Edinburgh), 1756.

The writer desires to record his indebtedness to the useful *Handbook and Directory of Old Scottish Clockmakers from* 1540 *to* 1850, by John Smith, Esq., published by William J. Hay, Esq., John Knox's House, Edinburgh, 1903. This volume is now out of print, and a new and enlarged edition containing no less than 2,700 names is shortly appearing. No student or collector of Scottish clocks can afford to be without this volume, as it is the only one dealing with its subject.

In regard to districts in England and Wales, there is an opportunity for local antiquarian societies to gather and tabulate county lists on the lines of this Scottish volume. The records of provincial makers are still exasperatingly incomplete.

There is the authoritative volume by the late F. J. Britten, *Old Clocks and Watches and their Makers*, with a list of over 10,000 names. But in the main these are of London makers.

**Character of Scottish Clocks.**—It is seldom that a clock by a Scottish maker is found to be cased in old oak. Most of the long-case clocks are of mahogany, which was not in general use till about 1740. It is true that there are exceptions, some few being found in lacquered or Dutch marquetry cases, but the majority are in mahogany.

In regard to clockmaking on a lower plane, there are the interesting clocks, with the works entirely constructed of wood, usually beech, as being the best wood adapted to cutting the teeth for the wheels; other woods used were holly and boxwood. Very few old examples now remain.

There seems, too, to have been a strong proclivity towards the musical clock. Several great makers produced fine examples of this class of clock which played popular airs. No doubt in the days of musical boxes, prior to the age of the gramophone, the great folk at Edinburgh, when the "Wizard of the North" enchanted society, had a penchant for these musical sweet-chiming clocks. Daniel Brown, of Mauchline, made the modest clock that stood in the cottage of Robert Burns; and James Gray, or John Smith, or Patrick Toshach, or one of the other clockmakers who made the hours "fading in music,"

ENLARGEMENT OF DIAL.

Showing maker's name, "Jos. Gibson, Ecclefechan." About 1750.

DIAL OF LONG PENDULUM CLOCK.

With single weight for going and striking trains. Spandrel ornaments finely cut and chased, representing the Four Seasons.

(*By courtesy of Edward Campbell, Esq., Glasgow.*)

WALL CLOCK.

Maker, George Graydon (Dublin). Date, about 1796.
With marquetry design showing volunteer in uniform, with G.R. on his cartouche box.

(*At the National Museum, Dublin.*)

may have constructed some musical marvel for the master of Abbotsford.

An interesting clock with the maker's name, Jos. Gibson, Ecclefechan, is illustrated (p. 267). It has a long pendulum and single weight for striking and going trains. The spandrels are finely cut and chased and represent the four seasons. This is a feature found on Dutch dials. In date this is about 1750. The enlargement of the dial (p. 267) shows that the engraver went wrong in his spacing. He had to put the last letter above the others. Indeed, it suggests that another hand than that which engraved the decoration and the name of the maker contributed the place. It is somewhat puzzling, and leads to conjecture as to its history. It is just such examples, out of the main stream of leading makers, which so often provide exceptional interest to the collector.

**Irish Clockmakers.**—The art of the clockmaker in Ireland, although having by no means lagged behind that of Scotland, has not received the attention of collectors and connoisseurs which it deserves.

Researches are being made, and new data are coming to hand which will assist the student to determine the period of Irish clockmakers' work. There are some 1,100 names already known of makers, and those interested await the results of close and painstaking investigation which will enable the record to be published.

By the kindness of Mr. Dudley Westropp, of the National Museum, Dublin, the following names are here given, tabulating a few of the leading Irish makers of the eighteenth century :—

George Aicken (Cork), 1770–95.
A clock by this maker is illustrated (p. 273).
Michael Archdekin (Dublin), 1769–1800.
Joseph Blundell (Dublin), 1703–32 (died).
Thomas Blundell (Dublin), 1733–75 (died).
Timothy Conway (Cork), 1783–1804 (died).
Thomas Coote (Dublin), 1733–47.
Hugh Cunningham (Dublin), 1755–77 (died).
George Furnace (Dublin), 1751–73.
Charles Gillespy (Dublin), 1747–71 (died).
Alexander Gordon (Dublin), 1756–87 (died).
There was an Alexander Gordon at Dundee, 1729. Maker of the first clock at Brechin Town Hall.

George Graydon (Dublin), 1764–1805 (died).
A clock by this maker is illustrated (p. 269).
Martin Kirkpatrick (Dublin), 1720–69 (died).
John Knox (Belfast), 1729–83.
Frederick May (Dublin), 1770–96.
Thomas Meeking (Dublin), 1682–1709 (died).
John Nelson (Dublin), 1786–1813.
James Pickering (Dublin), 1737–71 (died).
William Ross (Cork), 1764–1817.
Samuel Slocomb (Cork), 1735–50.
Edward Tounley (Dundalk), 1820–24.
Richard Wyatt (Dublin), 1731–55 (died).

These dates do not represent the makers' complete history. Some may have worked prior to the first date and after the last date, except when stated as having died then.

In regard to Belfast, the late Isaac W. Ward contributed some notes to the *Belfast Evening Telegraph* in 1909 on " Early Belfast Clock and Watchmakers," which enable some interesting particulars to be given. In 1791 one Job Rider announced that he had commenced business in Belfast, " where he makes clocks and watches of all kinds in the common manner with Harrison's and other modern improvements." It

MUSICAL CLOCK BY GEORGE AICKEN (CORK).

Date, 1770–95.

Lunette marked "Minuet, March, Jigg, Air, Minuet, Gavot." The indicator is pointing to "Air." Two subsidiary dials marked "Strike," "Not Strike," and "Chime," "Not Chime."

(*At National Museum, Dublin.*)

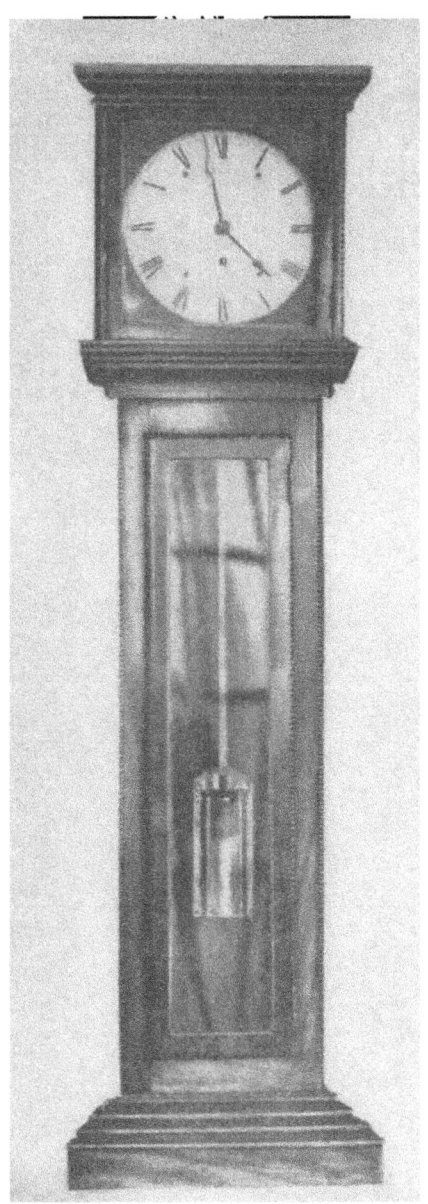

Made to hang from two rings at back of clock.
Maker, Sharp (Dublin). Early nineteenth century, showing French influence.
Height, 3 ft. 5½ in.  Width, 10⅞ in.  Base, 11¾ in.

*(By courtesy of Messrs. Harris & Sinclair, Dublin.)*

would appear that he had been to London, where possibly he was apprenticed, and had visited Dublin and Hillsborough. From 1805 to 1807 he was in partnership with R. L. Gardner. After 1807 he seems to have been associated with William Boyd.

Robert Neill, who was apprenticed to Job Rider in 1791, set up business in Belfast in 1803 and joined R. L. Gardner from 1809 to 1818. At this date the firm became known as Robert Neill & Sons. Robert Neill died in 1857. His descendants still carry on business at Belfast. Another Belfast maker was James Wilson, who worked in the middle of the eighteenth century. There is a record of a musical clock being advertised by him in 1755, which he had constructed to play a number of tunes.

The wall clock by George Graydon, of Dublin (illustrated p. 269), shows some interesting features. The circle round the dial is carved wood gilt; the dial itself is painted and very much cracked. The lower part is harewood inlaid. In date this example is about 1796, as it will be seen the volunteer in uniform on panel has G.R. on his cartouche-box.

The bracket clock by George Aicken, of Cork (illustrated p. 273), is of fine proportions and sound design. It has striking and chiming movements, and plays six tunes marked on lunette, "Minuet, March, Jigg, Air, Minuet, Gavot."

An early nineteenth-century clock by Sharp, of Dublin, is illustrated (p. 275). It is a miniature long-case clock, being only 3 feet $5\frac{1}{2}$ inches high. It is made to hang on the wall, as there are two rings at the back of the case for this purpose. Its glass door, showing the pendulum, indicates the French influence, which in the early nineteenth century made itself felt in Ireland as elsewhere.

In 1783 a company of Swiss watchmakers came to Ireland, and establishing themselves near Waterford, termed their settlement New Geneva. By 23 & 24 George III, 1784, they were granted power to assay gold and silver. An earlier Act of George II provided for only one standard of gold—22 carats. This new Act admitted three—22, 20, and 18 carats. These facilities were granted to encourage the manufacture of watches and watch-cases in Ireland. This Assay Office at New Geneva did not continue in operation more than six years.

The office at New Geneva had equal powers with the Dublin Assay Office. "The Assayer or Wardens are hereby required to make, on a plate of pewter or copper, impressions of such marks or punches, with the names and places of abode of the owner thereof, in a book or books to be carefully kept for that purpose, if such owners be resident at Dublin or New Geneva." Watches or other articles of gold and silver having the stamp "New Geneva" are in date 1784 to 1790.

# CHAPTER X

A FEW NOTES ON WATCHES

# CHAPTER X

### A FEW NOTES ON WATCHES

The age of Elizabeth — Early Stuart watches — Cromwellian period—Watches of the Restoration —The William and Mary watch—Eighteenth-century watches—Pinchbeck and the toy period—Battersea enamel and shagreen.

EARLY makers of English watches do not crowd the stage. On the Continent pocket clocks had had a long life before they made their appearance in this country. Queen Elizabeth had only one pair of silk stockings—she had been used to "cloth hose"—before her lady-in-waiting presented her with a pair straight from the Continent. Italian and French ideas were fast acclimatizing themselves here. Shakespeare laid many of his plays in Italy; the modern Elizabethan Englishman became quite Italian; the Queen read Tasso and Ariosto in the originals. In Germany the watch had taken various forms. The watchmakers of Nuremberg were renowned throughout Europe. "Nuremberg eggs," as they were styled, set the fashion for watches of all shapes suited to the conceits of the owner. Some were in the form of a skull, with appropriate mottoes concerning Time and Death; others were in the form of a cross, of a book, or shaped like a tulip or other flowers, or simulating butterflies and insects. The earliest styles had closed cases, these cases being subjected to various forms of ornament. The dial was not visible till the outer case was opened.

Collectors of watches are collecting something that is dead. The wheels are silent for ever. The interest lies in the remoteness of the conception of a pocket clock. Possibly there is no one alive who could now set the wheels into motion, as there are no designers who could originate the exquisite tracery and filigree work, the perfect enamelling and the delicacy of metal work these old watches exhibit.

They belong to a world apart. Clocks of old masters still carry on their functions: the hand still revolves in unison with the slow swing of the "royal pendulum." As timekeepers they equal most of the modern, and excel the cheap clock, hardly worth designating as a timekeeper. But the Swiss and the American factory-made watch, claiming no equality of artistic embellishment, have dethroned the antique watch in regard to accuracy. Curious and rare examples of the latter crowd the shelves of museums as being representative of that mysterious past when Time was of less moment than it is now. They belong to the age of the missal and the illuminated manuscript, and of the advent of printing with Caxton's well-balanced page. They

OLD ENGLISH WATCHES. SIXTEENTH AND SEVENTEENTH CENTURIES.

I. Elizabethan Watch, with carved and repoussé open-work design.

II. James I Watch. Dated 1620. Maker, Yate (London).

III. Cromwellian Plum-shaped Silver Watch, with crest engraved on case.

IV. Charles II Watch. 1660. Made by Snow of Lavington (near Bath).

V. William III Watch. Maker, Thomas Tompion. About 1690.

(*By courtesy of Percy Webster, Esq.*)

## A FEW NOTES ON WATCHES

are at variance with modernity. They were machines before the age of machinery—their very mechanism protests against being regarded as scientifically accurate. One lingers over their ornament with loving regard and forgets their purport. As timekeepers they fell short of the abbey clock, or of the sundial—a perennial stickler for truth when the sun shone. When the long pendulum, under the auspices of Christopher Huygens, commenced swinging, a timekeeper ready to hand eclipsed their gold and enamelled triumphs. But as fashionable baubles they had their continuous evolution, from Thomas Chamberlaine de Chelmisforde to Pinchbeck, and from Tompion to Eardley Norton. A considerable amount of ingenuity was given to producing examples of diminutive size which should perform adequately the correct functions of a timekeeper. But accuracy and scientific exactitude came late in the story of evolution. At length man's ingenuity triumphed. There are watches no larger than filberts which keep exact time, but there are thousands which do not.

The last popular watch, which our grandfathers termed a "turnip," was the stage prior to modern development, and at that stage collecting ends.

A scientific classification of watches would resolve itself under the following heads:—

I. *Early watches*, prior to the invention and general adoption of the fusee, that is, from about 1500 to 1540. This period would be further subdivided into (*a*) those with movements entirely of steel; (*b*) the next stage, with plates and pinions of brass and the wheels and pinions of steel; and the latest stage, (c), in which the plates and wheels were brass and the pinions of steel, as at the present day.

II. *Watches from about* 1540 *to* 1640, all having fusees, and being made of every conceivable shape and size: octagonal, oval, cruciform, in the shape of a book, and so on. The cases were sometimes of crystal or bloodstone, and enamelled designs and chased gold work were predominant features.

III. *Watches of the seventeenth century*, from 1610 to 1675, at which date the pendulum spring was invented. These are mainly round in shape, according to the fashion about 1620, which superseded the ancient quaint forms. The cases, both of silver and gold, were richly enamelled, and moving calendars and astronomical details were frequently made.

IV. *Late seventeenth and early eighteenth century watches.* These would embrace the period from 1675 to 1720, after the invention of the pendulum spring.

V. *The eighteenth century watch.* This should include all the improvements, changes in decorative style, and other details bringing the watch up to the threshold of the nineteenth century and modernity.

We can only indicate the type of watch as falling under the various periods, and specimens of the leading types are illustrated (pp. 283, 287).

The watches are numbered in the illustrations from one to ten, and can thus be easily identified by the reader.

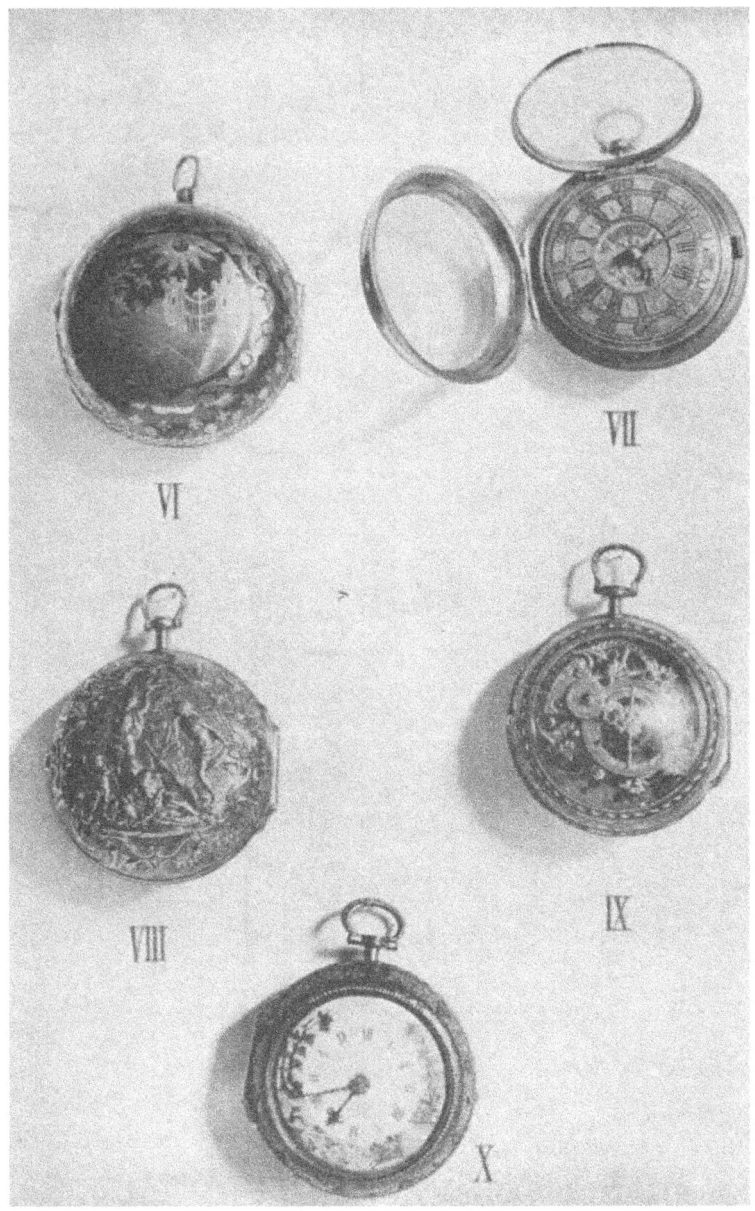

OLD ENGLISH WATCHES. EIGHTEENTH CENTURY.

VI. Watch with black piqué case. Maker, Peter Garron (about 1705).
VII. Early Georgian Watch with dark enamel dial. Maker, Duhamel. 1740.
VIII. Watch with repoussé work on case signed V. Haut. Maker, Haydon. 1731.
IX. Watch. Maker, Daniels of Leighton. About 1760.
X. Late Georgian Watch with dial and decorations in Battersea enamel and shagreen case.

(*By courtesy of Percy Webster, Esq.*)

# A FEW NOTES ON WATCHES 289

*No. 1* shows the character of an Elizabethan watch. The fine case shows the quality of the chased and repoussé open-work design.

*No. 2* is a James I oval watch, and the maker is Yate, of London. This watch is dated 1620, in the reign of James I, the year when the *Mayflower* sailed to America and New England was founded by those wise Puritans who foresaw the oncoming civil war of the next reign. The Earl of Ashburnham exhibited at the Stuart Exhibition in 1889 a gold watch which formerly belonged to Charles I, inscribed "Henricus Jones, Londini." Another maker of watches of this period is Edward East. The silver alarum clock given by Charles I on his way to execution to Thomas Herbert was made by Edward East. "Through the garden the King passed into the park, where making a stand, he asked Mr. Herbert the hour of the day: and taking the clock into his hand, gave it him, and bade him keep it in memory of him." This silver alarum watch is still treasured in the Mitford family.

*No. 3* is a Cromwellian silver watch, plum-shaped. As coats of arms were not so sinful as painted cherubs and stained-glass windows, this bauble with elaborately engraved crest survived the wreckers' despoiling hand. Cromwell himself boasted of a crest, and in some respects it resembled that used by royalty.

*No. 4* is a Restoration watch made by Snow, of Lavington, near Bath. It exhibits fine ornamentation and is a beautiful specimen of Late Stuart style when sumptuousness, under the guiding influence of the French Louis Quatorze grandeur, made itself felt in this country.

*No. 5* is worthy of respect and admiration as being the work of that great maker, Thomas Tompion. It is of the William and Mary period. The craftsman had arrived at the period of a scientific endeavour to create a perfect timekeeper. The case indicates utility; ornament is in due subjection. The Arabic figures showing the seconds on the dial should be observed.

*No. 6*, of which the back is shown, is a watch by Peter Garon. It is in black piqué case, finely decorated in a subdued and reticent manner. Peter Garon flourished between 1694 and 1706. But in that year, when Marlborough's campaigns were at their full height, poor Garon felt the stress of commercial depression and became bankrupt.

*No. 7*, showing the front and open case, is a fine watch by Duhamel, about 1740, bringing us to the days of George I and Walpole.

*No. 8*, with its fine broad repoussé case, is by Haydon, and the case is signed "V. Haut."

*No. 9* shows an illustration of the back, where the movement is visible. The maker of this is Daniels, of Leighton, 1760.

*No. 10* is by Kemp, London, and is decorated in Battersea enamel and shagreen. This brings us to the age of Pinchbeck, "the toyman in the Strand," and suggests the gewgaws and trifles, the enamelled heads for malacca canes, the snuff-boxes, and all the fashionable paraphernalia of a man about town. The watch in some respects had

CALENDAR WATCH. SEVENTEENTH CENTURY.

Maker, "Thomas Chamberline de Chelmisforde" (signature shown on right-hand illustration). The outer circle shows days of month. The indicator is pointing to 22nd.

*(By courtesy of Messrs. Mallett & Son, Bath.)*

begun to lose its old character and was again a toy.

Among interesting work is that of Thomas Chamberlaine de Chelmisforde. He worked in the brightest days of Charles I, when the arts were receiving stimulation from the Court. A new era seemed as though it might be about to dawn. The picture gallery of Charles I at Hampton Court showed his catholic taste, and his Queen, Henrietta Maria, was a patron of the arts. Vandyck and other great artists flocked to this country, and highly trained craftsmen commenced to build a reputation which later iconoclasts swept aside as of Baal.

In the watch illustrated by Thomas Chamberlaine there is something delightfully simple and chaste. He was a maker whose work promised much. There is a specimen of his work signed "Chamberlain Chelmisford" at the British Museum, but in the specimen illustrated the name is chased "Thomas Chamberlaine de Chelmisforde."

The study of watches of the various periods is a fascinating one. When the collector leaves the path of clocks, with their more Gargantuan proportions, to become a student of the intricacies of the art of the watchmaker as exemplified in some of his greatest triumphs, he has been enticed on a quest which is unending. No field in collecting and connoisseurship has claimed more devotees.

# INDEX

"Act of Parliament" clocks, so-called, 124
Adam style, its employment in the clock-case, 147
  Robert, clock-case by, illustrated, 139
Aicken, George (Cork), clock by, 277
Alarum clocks, 54
  and striking clocks, early, 32
Ale-house clocks, Oliver Goldsmith quoted, 127
American clocks—
  "Banjo clocks," 124
  Bracket clock, by Savin and Dyer (Boston), 198
  Lantern clock, with pendulum, 59
Anchor pendulum, the, 59
Arnold, John (Bodmin), 37, 212
Astronomical clock-dial, the, 28

Babylonian measurement of time, 28, 29, 30
Bacon, quoted, 53
Balance and weights prior to pendulum, 33
Barraud, clock by (1805), 203
Battersea enamel employed for watch-cases, 290

Beginners, hints for, 41
Belfast clocks and clockmakers, 272
Bewick, Thomas, engraver of clock-dials (1763–74), 215, 217
Biddell, clock by, 204
"Birdcage" clocks, 54
Böttger, his porcelain at Meissen, 109
Boulle, André Charles, and his marquetry, 72, 73, 111
Bracket clock, the, 179–204
  or wall clock, the, early use of, 46, 49
Brass lantern clock, the, 45–63
Bristol clock illustrated, 149
Britten, F. J., *Old Clocks and Clockmakers*, full lists of makers in, 37
Brownhill, Henry (Leeds), copper token of, 218

Cabrier, name falsely put on Dutch clocks, 36
Calendar watch illustrated, 291
Case, the, evolution of, 155
Catherine of Braganza, dowry of, 107
Centres of clock and watch making in 1797, 214

Chamber clocks an established feature in furniture, 192
Chamberlaine, Thomas, de Chelmisforde, watch by, 291
Charles I, watch belonging to, 289
Charles II, death-bed scene of, 50, 53
    Watch by Robert Hooke presented to, 36
Cherub head, the, a favourite ornament, 166
    Its use on clock-dial, 169
    Its use on Stuart furniture, 170
Cheshire clock-case, peculiarities of, 230
Chester, Bishop of (John Wilkins), quoted, 30
Chinese style of Chippendale, 91, 108
    Designs at Worcester, Bow, and Bristol porcelain factories, 108
    Taste, the *furore* in France and Holland, 108
Chintzes, the early character of, 111
Chippendale, his Chinese style, 91, 108
    His indebtedness to Marot, 155
    Style in clock cases, 136
Clockmakers' Company, 1704, transactions of, quoted, 36
    On fabrications of English work, 36
Clockmakers, the great English, 35
    English, full list of, 37
Clockmaking, decadence of, 38
    Personality in, 38, 39
Collecting period, the, 38
Collectors, hints for, foibles of, 39, 41
Colour *versus* form, 110

Cookworthy, William, his true porcelain at Plymouth, 109
Copper tokens of clockmakers illustrated, 218, 236
Cork, clocks and clockmakers at, 289
Cornwall clockmakers, list of, 241
Country marquetry, 60
Cromwellian "plum" watch illustrated, 283
Cumming, Alexander, clock by (1770), 203

Day and night, 27, 29
Day, the, its division into hours, 28
    Lunar, 29
    Mean solar, 28
Delft, Dutch, ornamentation of, used in marquetry, 98
Devon and Cornwall clockmakers, list of, 241
Dial, the—
    Brass, with silvered hour circle and engraved figures, 158
    Character of, 157
    Correct proportions of the, 165
    Early form of, 30
    Evolution of, 162, 165
    Iron painted ornament and figures, 158
    Position of maker's name on, 158, 161
Dickens, *Dombey and Son* quoted, 31
Domestic clock, the, 33
Draper, John (1703), dial of clock by, 158
Dublin clocks and clockmakers, 272
    National Museum, examples at, illustrated, 269, 273

# INDEX

Dutch clock panels imported, 97
  Delft ware, its imitation of porcelain, 111
  Fabrications of noted English makers, 36
  Influence on cabinet-maker, 67
  Influence on clockmaker, 217, 271
  Origin of long-case clock, 154
  Ornament found on clocks—
    Cupids and crown, 170
    Marquetry panels, 92
    Phases of moon, 217
    Spandrel with Seasons, 271
Dutton, Matthew, 37
  Thomas, 37
  William, 37

Earnshaw, Thomas (1750), 37, 212
East Anglian clockmakers, list of, 247
East, Edward, 37
East India Company, the Dutch, 107
  The English, 109
Ebsworth, John, 37
Edict of Nantes and its effect, 68, 90, 120
Edinburgh clocks and clockmakers, 261-265
Eighteenth century, best period of clockmaking in, 40
Elizabethan watch illustrated, 289
Ellicott, John (Bodmin), 212
English masters of clockmaking, the great, 35
  School of lacquered work, 114
Equation of time, 29
Evelyn, *Diary* of, quoted (1681), 107
Evolution of the English mantel clock, 186

Evolution of long-case clock, 153
  Base, its changing form, 155
  Dial, its character, 157
  Hands, their differing types, 174
  Spandrel, its ornamentation, 166
  Waist, its varying proportion, 155
Exeter clockmakers, list of, 241

Fleur-de-lis ornament on dial, 174
Foreign craftsmen working in England—
  Dutch marquetry workers, 83, 92
  French Huguenot cabinet-makers, 69, 90
  Italian glassworkers, 69
Form, changing, of hood, waist, and base, 155
  Innovations of, in clock-cases, 141
  *versus* colour, 111
French clocks and their influence, 147, 197, 278
  Influence on mantel clocks, 197
Fromanteel, Ahasuerus, pendulum introduced into England by, 37
  The family of, great clockmakers, 37
Furniture, influence of, on clock case, 141

Georgian clocks (1720-1830), 131
German school of marquetry, 72
Gibbons, Grinling, 121
Glasgow, example at Corporation Art Gallery illustrated, 259
Glass windows, when first used in coaches, 161
  Workers in London, seventeenth-century, 69

Goldsmith, Oliver, *Deserted Village* quoted, 127
Gordon, Patrick (Edinburgh), clock by, 261
Thomas (Edinburgh), 1668–1743, 261
Graham, George (1673–1751), 212
His evidence as to Robert Hooke's invention, 36
Grandfather clock, the, its Dutch origin, 74
Its long survival, 135
Its popularity, 135
Grant, John, 37
Inn clock by, illustrated, 125
Graydon, George (Dublin), clock by (1796), 277
Greek measurement of time, 28, 29

Halifax and district, list of clockmakers, 217
"Halifax" grandfather clocks, 217
Hampton Court, Dutch character of, 91
Protestant style of decoration at, 170
The work of Daniel Marot at, 91
The work of Sir Christopher Wren at, 91
Hands, the, evolution of, 174
Hour hand at first employed, 30, 157
Minute hand first added, 30, 158
Harris, Richard, clock by, at St. Paul's, Covent Garden, 35
Harrison, John, 37
His chronometer, 212
Hill, Thomas, clock by (1760), 197
Hogarth, William, the possibility of engraved clock-dials by, 161

Home Counties, the, list of clockmakers, 236
Hood, changing forms of the, 155
Hooke, Dr. Robert, his claim for invention of balance-spring for watches, 36
His inventions, 212
Watch by, presented to Charles II, 36
Hour, the, its division into minutes, 30, 158
Hours, division of day into, 30
Huguenot refugees settle in England, 68, 120
Huygens, Christopher, Dutch astronomer, his work, 33
His quarrel with Dr. Hooke, 36
Huygens, Dutch cabinet-maker, his imitations of Japanese lacquered panels, 111

Inlaid furniture, 70, 71
Inn clock, the, 124
Innovations of form in clock-cases, 141
Irish clockmakers, list of, 271, 272
Italian school of marquetry, 71

James I appoints Ramsay as "Clockmaker Extraordinary," 256
Japanese lacquer, specimens of, 106
Johnson, Thomas, clock by (1730), 191
Jones, Henry, Charles I watch made by, 289
Charles II clock by, 212

Kent and Sussex, clockmakers of, 247

# INDEX

Kew Gardens Botanical Museum, Japanese lacquer at, 106
Knibb, Joseph, father and son, 37
  Joseph (1670), 211
    Clocks by (1690), 191, 236, 241
    Copper token of (1677), 236
Knokmakers, the, of Scotland, 258

Labarte, *Arts of the Middle Ages* quoted, 33
Lac and its properties, 105
  Its introduction into England, 107
Lacquer—
  Chinese and Japanese origin of, 105, 106
  Dutch imitations, 110, 111
  English school of lacquer work, 118, 121
  French masters, 112
  Its use in the clock-case, 105
  Work—
    English school of, 114
    Foreign craftsmen in London, 120
    School of English amateurs, 121
Lacquered clock-case, its peculiarities, 112
  Panels imported from the East, 109
Lamb, Charles, quoted on sundials, 162
  Name falsely put on Dutch clocks, 36
Lancashire clock-case, peculiarities of, 230
  Clockmakers, list of, 230
Lantern clock—
  Early form, 45
  Its similarity to ship's lantern, 46
Lilly, *Life and Times* quoted, 256

Liverpool and district, list of clockmakers, 224
Long-case clock—
  Dutch origin of, 154
  Evolution of the, 153
  Georgian period, the, 131
  Lacquer period, the, 105
  Stability of the, 132
  Veneer and marquetry period, the, 67
Loomes, Thomas, clock by, 191
Lovelace, Jacob (Exeter), 212, 242
Lowestoft china, so-called, with Dutch inscription, 173
Lunar day, the, 29
Lunette, the use of the, in dial and case, 158
Lustre ware clock vase, Staffordshire, 198

Macaulay, his account of death of Charles II, 50, 53
Mahogany long cases, the period of, 136
Makers, old, their personality given to clocks, 38
Mantel clocks, the English character of, 185
Marot, Daniel, his work at Hampton Court, 90, 91
  Designs of long-case clocks, 155
Marquetry—
  Country cabinet-makers' use of, 84
  Decadence of, 100
  Definition of, 71
  Dutch school of, 79
  Early English attempt at, 84
  Finest period, 40, 79, 83
  Foreign influence on English art, 79

Marquetry (*continued*)—
 German school of, 72
 Imported sheets, frequent use of, 84, 97
 Italian school of, 71
 Provincial, 60
 Revival of, Sheraton period, 123, 147
 Veneer, the use of, with, 74
Martin, Sieur Simon Etienne, his varnish, 112
Mary, Queen, and Hampton Court, 98, 170
Massy, Henry (1680), dial of clock by, 158
Mean time, 29
Mechanism of clocks, early, 32
Midlands, list of clockmakers in the, 230
Mills, Humphry, Edinburgh (1661), 261
 Richard, Edinburgh (1678–1710), 261
Minute, the, its division into seconds, 30
Mudge, Thomas, Exeter (1715), 37, 212
Musical clock attributed to Rimbault, 142
 by George Aicken, Cork, 277

Name of maker, position on dial, 161
Names found on dials, origin of, 213
Nantes, Edict of, and its effect, 68, 120
Newcastle-upon-Tyne, list of makers, 215
New Geneva (near Waterford), Irish watchmaking centre at, 278
 Silver assayed at, 278

New York Metropolitan Art Museum, clocks illustrated, 57, 193
Nineteenth century, best period of clockmaking in, 40
 Long-case clock of the, 147
North of England, list of clockmakers, 215
Nottingham clockmakers, list of, 235
Numerals on dial, note on, 158, 165

Painted furniture simulating lacquer work, 123
Panels, lacquered, imported from the East, 109
 Marquetry, their use in clock-case, 97
"Parliament" clocks, so-called, 124
Pendulum, the—
 Advent of, 50
 Early studies relating to, 154
 First introduction of, 33
 Introduced into England by Fromanteel, 37
 Length of, determined by longitude, 179
 Types of—the anchor, 59; the "royal" or long, 33; the short, its position at front of dial, 33
Pepys' *Diary* quoted (1667), 161
Personal clock, the, 34
Personality in clockmaking, 38
Pinchbeck, Christopher, 37
 Period of watches, 290
Pitt, his tax on clocks (1797), 124
Pope, *Essay on Criticism* quoted, 31
Porcelain, true, its introduction into Europe, 109
Poy, Godfrey, clock by (1745), 192
Pre-pendulum clocks, 33

# INDEX

Provincial clocks and makers, 211
  Makers, some great, 211

Quare, name falsely put on Dutch clocks, 36
Queen Mary, her influence in rebuilding Hampton Court, 98

Ramsay, David, 255; watch signed by, 257
Réfugié, le style, its introduction into England, 90
Regulator clock, the, 148
Repairs, ignorant restoration to be avoided, 42
Riesener, the marquetry of, 111
Rimbault, Stephen, 37
  Noteworthy for musical clocks, 142, 147
Roentgen, David, the marquetry of, 111

Science, the dawn of, 35
Scott, Sir Walter, *Fortunes of Nigel* quoted, 255
Scottish clocks, 255
  Character of, 266
  Makers, eighteenth century, list of, 261, 262
  Second, the, the second division of the hour, 30
  Hand, the, 30
  Seventeenth century, dawn of science in the, 35
  Types of lantern clock, 53
  Watches, 286, 287
Shagreen cases to watches, 290
Shakespeare, *As you like it* quoted, 162
  *King John* quoted, 32
Sheraton style in clock-cases, 147

Spandrel ornament on clock-dial—
  Artistic difficulty of, 166
  Cherub head style, 166, 169
  Cupids and crown style, 170
Spanish proverb quoted, 185
Specialization of clockmaking, 37
Spring, the, its early use as a motive power, 32
Staffordshire earthenware clock vase, 198
Stalker and Parker, treatise on "japanning" (1688), 122
Striking and alarum clocks, early, 32
Strowbridge (Dawlish), clock by, 204
  Clock repaired by, 247
Stuart and Tudor ages compared, 35
Sundial, the, and its tradition, 162
  Time, 29
Sussex, clockmakers of, 247
  Clock (Ashburnham) illustrated, 243
Swiss watchmakers settled in Ireland (1784–90), 278

Table clocks, great variety of, 185
Time, apparent and mean, equation of, 29
  and its measurement, 27
  Babylonian method of reckoning, 28, 29, 30
Tokens, copper, of clockmakers illustrated, 218, 236
Tombstones, ornament on, indicative of contemporary styles, 157
Tomlinson, William, 37
Tompion, Thomas (1671–1713), 212, 236
  Name of, falsely put on Dutch clocks, 36
Tudor and Stuart ages compared, 35

# INDEX

Veneer and marquetry, the use of, 74
  Definition of, 69
  Modern delicacy of, 69
Verge escapement of old clocks, 33
Vulliamy, Benjamin, 37
  Benjamin Lewis, 37
  Justin, 37

Wales, clocks made in, 248
Wall clock, early use of, 46, 49
  Inn clock illustrated, 125
  Irish wall clock illustrated, 277
Wall-paper—
  Early use of in England, 99
  Period in marquetry, 99
  Repeat design of, on marquetry, 100
Walnut period of long case, 135, 136
Watches, Old English—
  Battersea enamel, 290
  Cromwellian, 289
  Early Stuart, 289
  Eighteenth-century, 290
  Elizabethan, 289
  Pinchbeck period, 290
  Typical English described, 285, 286
  William and Mary, 290

Watches, Liverpool and district famous for, 224
Waterford, Swiss watchmakers at, 278
Watson, Sam (Coventry), clock by (1687), 186
Webster's *New International Dictionary* quoted, 30
Wedgwood medallions as ornaments to clock-case, 204
Welsh clocks and makers, 248
West Country clockmakers, list of, 241
Wilkins, John, Bishop of Chester, quoted, 30
William and Mary period of decoration, 92, 97, 98
Windmills, name falsely put on Dutch clocks, 36
Woodcarvers at Hampton Court, 170
Wooden works of clocks, 266
Wren, Sir Christopher, his work at, Hampton Court, 91

Yorkshire clock-case, peculiarities of, 223, 229
  Clockmakers, 217

Zoffany, clock-cases decorated by, 142

www.ingramcontent.com/pod-product-compliance
Lightning Source LLC
Chambersburg PA
CBHW031422150426
43191CB00006B/366